Contents

CONTENTS

Acknowledgements

The authors and publisher would like to thank the following individuals and organisations for permission to reproduce photographs and other copyright material:

Ace Photos – page 6 (right), 150, 180, 181
Advertising Archives – page 28
Advertising Standards Authority – page 58 (top)
Alton Towers – page 49, 195 (bottom)
Arsenal Football Club Plc – page 189, 196, 197
Birds Eye Walls Ltd – page 51
BMW Group – page 147
Boots The Chemists – page 97, 172
BP plc – page 7
Cadbury Schweppes plc – page 83, 99
Collections/John Callan – page 30
Collections/Richard Davis – page 4 (left)
Collections/Eric Lewis – page 94
Collections/Nick Oakes – page 111
Co-Operative Group Ltd – page 25
Costco – page 88
Empics – page 50 (bottom)
English Riviera Tourist Board – page 48 (top)
English Tourism Council – page 62
Environmental Images – page 42
Financial Times – page 142
Ford Motor Company – page 70, 159
FPD Savills Ltd – page 165
GlaxoSmithKline – page 59
Sally & Richard Greenhill – page 48 (bottom), 130, 137
Greggs plc – page 139, 157
Guardian Newspapers – page 159, 161
Halfords Ltd – page 95
Holland & Barrett Retail Ltd – page 53
IKEA – page 68 (bottom right)
Impact/Piers Cavendish – page 140
Impact/Tony Page – page 4 (middle)

John Lewis Partnership – page 109
Keith Pattinson Ltd – page 142
Kwik-Fit Holdings Plc – page 119
Lectra Systems – page 158
Longhirst Hall – page 112
McDonalds Restaurants Ltd – page 36, 37, 75, 126, 127
Mars UK Ltd – page 75
Meadowhall Shopping Centre – page 38, 87
Morgan Car Company – page 136
Nestlé UK Ltd – page 29, 71, 162, 182
Nissan – page 10
Ntl – page 93
Powerstock/Zefa – page 20
Raleigh Industries Ltd – page 18 (top), 50 (top)
Rex Features – page 44, 96
Rhys Davies Freight Logistics – page 91
River Island – page 18 (bottom)
Sainsbury's Supermarkets Ltd – page 9, 73
Roger Scruton – page 4 (bottom), 26 (top), 26 (bottom), 54, 58 (bottom), 61, 68 (bottom middle), 72, 75, 92 (bottom), 186, 195 (top)
Snackhouse Plc – page 71
Telegraph Colour Library – page 34, 118, 182
Tesco – page 141
Times Newspapers Ltd (22.11.00, 26.01.01, 25.11.00) – page 11, 121, 129
TV Choice – page 67
Virgin Group Ltd – page 13, 21, 155
Vodafone – page 92 (top)
Volkswagen – page 68 (middle right)
Walkers Crisps Ltd – page 68 (top right), 85
John Walmsley – page 4 (top), 4 (middle)
Warburtons Ltd – page 139

Every effort has been made to contact copyright holders of material published in this book. We would be glad to hear from unacknowledged sources at the first opportunity.

The authors would also like to thank Pat Bond.

How to use this book

This book has been designed to help you work towards your GCSE Business Studies exam. It will also be helpful for other business courses such as GNVQ. IT tasks have been included so you can show your IT skills in the presentation of your work.

Each unit of work is divided into sections. These sections use businesses to illustrate the new topics you are learning about. In each section there are explanations of different business theories and concepts. These will help you understand how business works and some of the decisions that business people have to make.

The following elements are also included within the units to provide you with practice and extra information.

TALK IT OVER

These are questions which will encourage you to think about the theory in each topic.

BUSINESS IN PRACTICE

An example of a business situation or problem, usually based on real companies. This will help you apply the theory you are studying. At the end of each case study there are questions for you to answer.

KEY POINTS

At the end of each topic there is a list of key points that you should have learnt. These points will be useful when you are revising for your examinations.

TEST YOUR UNDERSTANDING

At the end of a group of topics there is a series of exam-type questions, including extension questions. These are short questions which test your knowledge and understanding of the facts contained in the topics.

CASE STUDY

An example of a business situation or problem, usually based on real companies. This will help you understand the new ideas you are studying. At the end of each case study there are questions for you to answer.

EXAM PRACTICE

The review sections contain structured questions, including extension questions, which are similar to those found on any GCSE examination paper. These questions give you the chance to practise thinking and apply the theory you have learnt to business situations.

Business and its Environment

TOPIC 1 Consumers, suppliers, goods and services

CONSUMER NEEDS AND WANTS

Businesses exist to make a profit by providing things that people **need** and **want**. From the day we are born we all need food, drink, shelter, warmth and clothes, if we are to survive, so there are businesses that provide us with food, drink, houses and clothes. Some businesses make the things and others sell them – for instance, Kellogg's makes cornflakes, and Sainsbury's sells them.

There are also businesses which support the making and selling of goods, for example transport companies to deliver the raw materials to the factory and finished goods to the customer, and banks and insurance companies to provide services to the businesses.

There are other things we would *like*, to make our lives more enjoyable, but which are not essential, such as a holiday, a computer, or a visit to the cinema.

CHOICES

We do not have an unlimited amount of money, so we must make **choices** about what we buy. These decisions usually involve choosing between two or more alternatives.

Businesses and governments have to make similar choices. A business may have to decide which is more important: a new piece of machinery or an extra member of staff. The government has to set its priorities when spending its income each year. Which is more important: education or social services?

The cost of making a particular decision is known as the **opportunity cost**. If you only have enough money to buy *either* a computer game *or* a CD, the opportunity cost of choosing the computer game is the CD – by buying the game, you give up the opportunity to buy the CD.

TALK IT OVER

What choices have you made recently?

GOODS AND SERVICES

We saw earlier that Kellogg's makes cornflakes for its customers, and Sainsbury's sells food to its customers. The cornflakes that Kellogg's makes are **goods**. When Sainsbury's sells the cornflakes it is providing the **service** of bringing the goods near to where we live.

Goods are physical things that can be bought, such as a mountain bike or a CD. Services are non-physical items that can be bought, such as having a driving lesson or going to the dentist.

Anyone who buys goods or services for their own use is called a **consumer**. We are all consumers. The consumer goods that we buy can be:

◆ **consumer durables** – items that can be used over and over again (for example, a computer or a pair of trainers)

◆ for **single use** – items that can be used only once (for example, a packet of crisps or a disposable camera).

Goods and services

 TALK IT OVER

How many consumer durables do you own?

THE IMPORTANCE OF DECISIONS

Faced with the same alternatives, not all consumers will make the same choice – nor will all businesses, nor all governments. Consumers, businesses and governments make decisions on *what they think is best for them in their situation.*

Businesses are constantly making decisions about issues such as what to produce, the price to charge, buying machinery, advertising and investment. This is one of the most important aspects of studying Business Studies – using theory to help understand, explain and evaluate business decisions.

KEY POINTS

■ **Needs** – what we need to survive, e.g.
– food
– drink
– shelter.

■ **Wants** – what we would like but do not need for survival, e.g.
– a holiday
– a computer.

■ **Business activity** – providing goods and services to satisfy consumer needs and wants.

■ **Opportunity cost** – the cost of rejecting the alternatives when making choices.

■ **Goods** – physical objects that can be bought.

■ **Services** – non-physical things that can be bought.

■ **Consumer durables** – goods that can be used over and over again, e.g.
– a television
– a coat.

■ **Single-use items** – goods that can be used only once, e.g.
– a bottle of milk
– a chocolate bar.

■ **Business decision-making** – choosing between different possible courses of action.

Different countries have different ways of deciding which goods and services are provided for consumers. There are three types of **economy**: the **market economy**, the **planned** or **command economy**, and the **mixed economy**.

All countries operate a mixture of market and planned economies, with countries such as the USA tending more towards a market economy than, for instance, France or Germany.

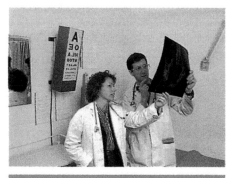

In the UK the National Health Service is run by the government

MARKET ECONOMY

In a **market economy** consumers decide which goods and services they want, and businesses provide them. Almost all businesses in a market economy are privately owned. The main features of a market economy are:

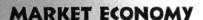

- consumer demand dictates which goods and services the businesses will supply
- the businesses are there to make a profit
- the number of goods and services provided is decided through the **price system** (the **market price**) – anyone who is willing and able to pay the prices can buy goods and services
- most of the factors of production – land, labour, capital – are privately owned.

Most education in the UK is also run by the government

Advantages of a market economy

- Any **entrepreneur** (business person) with an idea for a product or service can start up a business if the necessary finance is available.
- **Competition** between businesses encourages greater efficiency and the development of new products.
- There is the opportunity to make large profits.
- Prices help to match demand and supply so that consumers do not have shortages.

 TALK IT OVER

What happens to the price of a good when demand increases?

Most goods and services are provided by private businesses – in a mixed economy, goods and services are provided by the government as well as by private businesses

Disadvantages of a market economy

◆ Businesses will not provide goods or services if they cannot make a profit from them.

◆ Monopolies can be created and they can then control how much is made and the prices to be charged.

◆ Too much competition can be wasteful as more goods may be made than the consumers want.

PLANNED ECONOMY

In a **planned** (or **command**) **economy** the government or state owns most of the businesses and controls the country's resources. The government decides what, and how much, will be produced; and then businesses have to meet these targets. The consumer has no say in decisions about goods or services. Many countries, including Russia, China, Cuba and most East European countries, used to have planned economies, but now most of these have changed and have mixed economies.

MIXED ECONOMY

A **mixed economy** is a combination of the market economy and the planned economy. Some decisions are made between the consumers and the businesses. Others are made by the government. In the UK we have a mixed economy. The majority of businesses are owned by private individuals, called **entrepreneurs**. Some businesses, such as the Post Office, the National Health Service and most education services, are owned and run by the government.

KEY POINTS

■ The three main types of economy are:
– market
– planned/command
– mixed.

■ A **market economy** is controlled by:
– consumer demand
– business.

■ A **planned/command economy** is controlled by:
– government.

■ A **mixed economy** is controlled by:
– government
– consumer demand
– business.

 TALK IT OVER

Why does the government provide most of the health care in the UK?

 BUSINESS IN PRACTICE

When Sony Playstation 2 hit Britain, shortages sparked an immediate black market trade. Consoles retailing for £299 were being sold on the Internet for as much as £1000.

Sony introduced an order-only system for the first batch of machines, and this meant that stocks sold out long before consoles reached the shops. Sony denied making the situation worse by releasing only 165 000 consoles.

The Consumers' Association is expecting a wave of ads in local papers offering consoles at exorbitant prices.

Adapted from Craig Clarke: 'Fans pay £1000 to get Sony consoles', in *The Times*, 25.11.00

 TALK IT OVER

How has the market economy contributed to the high price of a Sony console?

TOPIC 3 Production

Production involves using the **factors of production** to make goods and to provide services. The four important resources that are the factors of production are:

- land – to build shops and factories and provide natural resources such as oil and crops
- labour – people involved in production, producing the goods or providing the service
- capital – to finance the business, machinery and buildings
- enterprise – bringing together the factors of production and taking risks with ideas: people who do this are called **entrepreneurs**.

Crisps were originally unflavoured, and came with some salt in a twist of blue paper. An entrepreneur had the idea of producing crisps ready-salted. The entrepreneur needed:

- capital to buy machinery and buildings
- land to provide potatoes and other ingredients
- labour to make the crisps.

Factors of production

TYPES OF PRODUCTION

Business activity can be organised into three categories:
- primary production
- secondary production
- tertiary production.

Primary

Extraction of raw materials

Secondary

Turning raw materials into finished goods

Tertiary

Providing services

PRIMARY PRODUCTION

The first stage of the production process is where raw materials and natural resources are farmed or extracted from the land or sea, for example by growing crops, rearing livestock, or extracting minerals such as oil and coal.

SECONDARY PRODUCTION

The second stage of the production process turns these raw materials and natural resources into finished products. Examples of secondary production are manufacturing, assembly and construction, such as car manufacture or house building.

TERTIARY PRODUCTION

Businesses involved in the third stage of the production process provide services. Examples of tertiary production are:

◆ businesses that provide services to industry and individuals, such as banking or insurance
◆ businesses that provide services directly to the consumer, such as hairdressing, travel agencies or football clubs
◆ services to the state such as education (provided by teachers), law and order (provided by the police force), or the National Health Service (provided by doctors and nurses).

KEY POINTS

■ The three types of business activity are:
 – **primary production**: extracting raw materials and natural resources from the land or sea
 – **secondary production**: turning the raw materials and natural resources into finished goods
 – **tertiary production**: providing services.

■ The four **factors of production** are:
 – **land**: siting premises and providing raw materials
 – **labour**: producing goods and providing services
 – **capital**: financing the business
 – **enterprise**: taking risks and bringing together the other factors of production.

BUSINESS IN PRACTICE

BP Amoco plc operates in Europe, North and South America, Australia and Africa. The main business activities are exploration and production of crude oil and natural gas, refining, and manufacturing petrochemicals. These products are marketed and transported all over the world. BP owns almost 30 000 service stations.

 TALK IT OVER
What is BP's involvement in primary, secondary and tertiary production?

The groups of people involved in business activity are often called **stakeholders** because they have an interest, or stake, in the business. Stakeholders may be:

- owners
- managers
- employees
- consumers
- government
- community.

Owners

OWNERS

Owners put their own money into a business. They have a say in the decision-making in the business, and a share of the profits.

MANAGERS

Managers are people who are employed by the owners to oversee the day-to-day running of the business. They put the owners' decisions into practice.

Managers

In small businesses, such as **sole traders**, the owner is often also the manager and makes all decisions. In larger businesses, such as **partnerships** or **limited companies**, managers may be experts in specific areas such as **marketing** or **finance**. You can learn more about the different types of businesses in Unit 1, Topics 6–10.

EMPLOYEES

Employees are paid to work for the business, doing a specific job. The employees' stake is the money in the form of the pay they receive, which they can spend on goods and services.

Employees

CONSUMERS

Consumers buy the goods and services produced. If businesses do not provide what consumers want, they will quickly be in financial difficulties.

Consumers

GOVERNMENT

The **government** wants business to be successful to provide wealth for the country. Business is influenced by the laws the government introduces.

Government

The stakeholders of a supermarket

TALK IT OVER

Why might owners and employees have different objectives?

COMMUNITY

Businesses are important to communities because they provide employment, however they can damage a community's environment by creating air, noise and visual pollution.

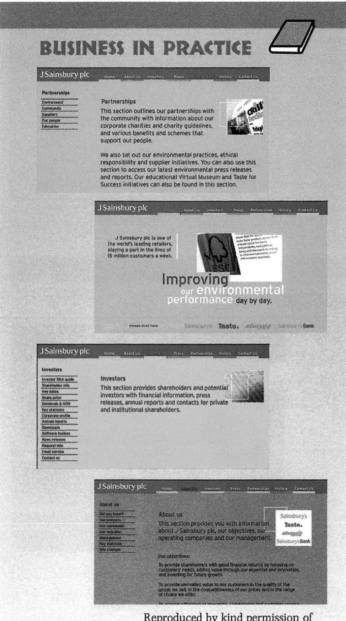

Reproduced by kind permission of
Sainsbury's Supermarkets Ltd

TALK IT OVER

Why do the directors of Sainsbury's want to become involved with the community?

KEY POINTS

The main groups of people involved in business activity are:

- **owners** – people who invest their own money in starting a business

- **managers** – people employed to control the general running of a company

- **employees** – people who perform specific roles within a company in return for pay

- **consumers** – people who buy goods and services for their own use

- **government** – elected members of parliament who run the country

- **community** – people and organisations in a local area.

TEST YOUR UNDERSTANDING

TOPICS 1–4

1 What is business activity?

2 Explain the difference between a *need* and a *want*.

3 Use an example to explain the term *opportunity cost*.

4 Describe a mixed economy.

5 Explain what an *entrepreneur* does.

6 Why is capital important to a business?

7 Describe primary production, using an example.

8 Give three examples of secondary production.

9 Describe the range of services included in the tertiary sector.

10 Who might be the stakeholders of a business? For each stakeholder, state their interest in the business.

CASE STUDY

Wearside heaved a sigh of relief yesterday at the news that the new Nissan Micra is to be built at the company's plant in Sunderland.

More than 1200 jobs were on the line as the Japanese owners hovered between the Sunderland assembly line and the Renault plant at Flins in France. A £40 million EU grant helped to tip the balance to the North East.

Colin Anderson, leader of Sunderland City Council, said, 'The hard work of the people at the plant has won through in the end. The management has also played its part by reducing the plant's costs by 30%.'

'Nissan came to Sunderland at a time when things were desperate. Unemployment was at a high level and the traditional industries were dying out. The workforce made Nissan the most productive car plant in the Western world.'

Fraser Kemp, Labour MP, said, 'It is good news not just for Wearside and the North East but for Britain as a whole.'

Hugh Morgan-Williams, regional director of the CBI, said 'This is a fantastic decision for Nissan and for British industry.'

Arthur Cutting, maintenance technician and member of the company council, said, 'All the weight that has been on the workers' shoulders has been lifted. People with mortgages, debts and families to look after have had a stressful few months.'

John Cushnaghan, managing director of Nissan UK, said, 'It is the attitude and the commitment of the excellent workforce who make Sunderland by far the most efficient car plant in Europe.'

Adapted from Paul Wilkinson: 'North East celebrates Nissan decision', *The Times*, 26.1.01

1 To which sector of production does Nissan belong?

2 What was the opportunity cost of Nissan building the Micra in Sunderland?

3 What might Nissan have considered when making the decision?

4 Explain why labour seems to have been the most influential factor of production in the decision.

5 Identify and explain the interests of all the stakeholders in Nissan.

EXAM PRACTICE

Joe James, aged 48 years, was made redundant from his job as a car salesman. He decided to start his own business. Joe is a keen angler and opened a shop, with an attached workshop where he could repair fishing tackle. As well as taking in repairs the shop sells a range of fishing tackle.

1 What might be the reasons for Joe's decision to start his own business? [3 marks]

2 Describe *two* business decisions Joe might have to make during the first year of his shop being open. [2 marks]

3 Explain whether Joe is producing a good or providing a service. Give reasons for your answer. [3 marks]

4 Describe two factors of production that Joe will need. [4 marks]

5 Explain how starting the business will benefit: (a) consumers; (b) the local community. [8 marks]

Joe James, aged 48 years, was made redundant from his job as a car salesman. He decided to start his own business. Joe is a keen angler and opened a shop, with an attached workshop where he could make flies for fishing. The shop sells a range of fishing tackle alongside the hand-made flies.

1 What is the opportunity cost of Joe's decision? Give reasons to support your answer. [4 marks]

2 Explain where Joe's business is in the chain of production. [4 marks]

3 Discuss the factors of production that Joe will need in order to start and run his new business. [12 marks]

Any entrepreneur starting up a business has a number of goals that he or she wants to achieve. These are called **objectives**. Over time, the objectives of a business can change as the business grows or faces difficulties.

The main objective of any business is to make a **profit**. The owners will expect some return on the money they have invested in the business. However, if the business is new or has recently been expanded, then the main objective will be **survival**. Survival might be the main objective if the economy is experiencing recession with high unemployment. Some owners start their businesses to follow an **interest** – examples include creative people, such as artists, and people who love animals, such as dog breeders.

When a business is surviving, the owners will probably want the business to make more profit by **increasing sales**. The objective might be to increase sales to become the biggest business in the industry and to have the biggest **market share**. Many managers want the business to **grow** and open several branches or employ lots of workers, as this will probably improve their salaries and their job security. The owners might decide that they will beat their competition by having an excellent **reputation**.

A business may be started because the owner wants to be **independent** instead of working for someone else, or to give **customer satisfaction** by providing an excellent product or service. An owner may gain satisfaction by **providing employment** for people.

Some owners start their business to follow an interest

STAKEHOLDERS

The interests of **stakeholders** will affect business objectives, depending on the amount of influence they have. Often the objectives of different groups are in conflict. For example:

- the *owners* of a sportswear manufacturer might want to introduce computerised manufacturing and sales over the Internet, believing that this would maximise profits and dividends
- the *managers* might want to introduce sales over the Internet because this would increase market

 TALK IT OVER

What do you think are the objectives of some of the businesses you know?

 TALK IT OVER

How might the stakeholders in Marks & Spencer plc react to the closure of some of its European stores?

share, create a good reputation, and probably increase their salaries and career development; but they might not want to introduce computerised manufacturing, because this could cause industrial action and make managing difficult

◆ the *workers* might not want any change, as either dispute could involve job losses

◆ the *customers* (the retailers) might want computerised manufacturing, which would reduce prices; but not Internet sales, as they would then lose customers

◆ *consumers* might want computerised manufacturing as this might lead to lower prices and increased quality, *and* sales over the Internet which would make their purchases easier.

BENEFITS OF BUSINESS GROWTH

There are definite advantages to being a large business when it comes to **expansion** and **growth**:

◆ It is easier to borrow money for growth, as the large business is seen as a better **risk**.

◆ Large businesses have great **influence** around the world, with other businesses and with governments.

◆ Large businesses are better able to develop new ideas as more money is available for **research** and **development**.

◆ Large businesses can take advantage of **economies of scale** which means that average costs fall (Unit 4, Topic 9).

KEY POINTS

As businesses grow they gain advantages:

■ they are seen as less of a **risk** and so find it easier to raise **capital**

■ as they get larger their **influence** on other businesses and even governments increases

■ they can spend more time and money on developing new ideas

■ they gain **economies of scale**.

BUSINESS IN PRACTICE

Most large businesses, even the multinationals, can often be traced back to a single owner starting up a small business with a good idea.

Richard Branson is such a person. His first business venture started in January 1968, with the first issue of his student magazine. Two years later he started the Virgin mail-order operation, and in 1971 he opened his first record shop in Oxford Street. Since then the Virgin Group of companies has grown and grown.

 ### TALK IT OVER

Could you do what Richard Branson did? What kind of person must he be?

There are five main types of business organisation:
- sole traders
- partnerships
- private limited companies
- public limited companies
- co-operatives.

The way a business is organised and run depends upon the type of business.

A sole trader

WHAT IS A SOLE TRADER?

The sole trader type of business is owned by one person. The sole trader can employ people, but these employees are unlikely to be involved in the control, financing, or decision-making of the business. In your area, people such as electricians, taxi drivers, hairdressers, and guest-house owners are probably sole traders.

In the UK, the sole trader is the most common form of business ownership, with over three million people in business as sole traders. Many young people today are setting up their own businesses, helped by start-up grants from central government or charities such as the Prince's Trust.

The sole trader has to make all the decisions about running the business. He or she keeps all of the profits. It is more difficult to raise large amounts of money from loans, as sole traders are seen as being more of a risk than large businesses. Sole traders often have to use their own money or borrow from family or friends to start up the business. As a result, most sole traders are small businesses.

SETTING UP AS A SOLE TRADER

This is a simple process, as few regulations are involved.

You will need to decide on a name for your business. You may need to find business premises. You will have to raise the capital necessary to start the business. You will have to decide whether or not you want to employ any people to help you run the

BUSINESS IN PRACTICE

Thornton Cole has a painting and decorating business. He is a sole trader and has run his own business for five years. His customers include bigger businesses, such as builders, and house owners and tenants. Thornton sometimes has contracts with hospitals and schools.

Thornton works every day of the week. He never starts any later than 8 am, and he works as long as it takes to finish the job. In the evenings he does his accounts and prepares estimates.

Usually Thornton works alone, but he knows of painters he can employ temporarily if needed.

 TALK IT OVER

Explain why Thornton Cole describes himself as a 'happy man'.

business. You need to be able to keep the **accounts** accurately yourself, or find an accountant who will do them for you. Each year the accounts must be sent to the Inland Revenue (the government agency that collects income tax).

ADVANTAGES

- This kind of business is easy to set up – there are no complicated forms or procedures to follow.
- Sole traders can make decisions quickly as they do not have to get agreement from anyone else.
- Sole traders usually need less capital to set up.
- All the profits can be kept by sole traders, which motivates them to work harder.
- The sole trader can offer the personal attention and service to customers that a large company is unable to provide.
- The sole trader does not have to tell anyone except the Inland Revenue any information about the state of the business.
- Sole traders are their own bosses, and can choose their own working hours and holidays.

 TALK IT OVER

What do you think is the biggest advantage of being a sole trader?

DISADVANTAGES

- Sole traders have **unlimited liability**. This means that the owner may have to sell personal possessions to pay off any debts the business might have run up.
- Small businesses are seen as more of a risk, so it can sometimes be difficult to raise money to start a business or to expand later on.
- Ill-health and holidays may affect the business as there is no one to take over and run it. Often the business will have to close for this period of time.
- The sole trader has no one with whom to discuss business decisions.
- Sole traders may find it difficult to compete with large businesses in terms of price.

KEY POINTS

- A business is called a **sole trader** when:
  - there is only one owner
  - the owner has to make all the decisions
  - the owner has unlimited liability.
- **Unlimited liability** – the owner is personally responsible for all the debts of the business.
- To be successful a sole trader needs:
  - a desirable product or service
  - a name for the business
  - business premises
  - starting capital
  - accurate financial records
  - satisfied customers to tell other potential customers
  - possibly to employ other staff.

 TALK IT OVER

Think of a successful sole trader you know and explain why you think they have been successful.

WHAT IS A PARTNERSHIP?

A partnership involves between 2 and 20 people, who are the owners of the business. Partnerships are common in businesses that involve professionals such as doctors, dentists, accountants and solicitors.

The partners may specialise within the business – in a firm of solicitors, for example, different partners may specialise in civil, criminal or commercial law.

Like the sole trader, partnerships have unlimited liability – if the business fails, the partners are all personally liable for the debts of the business. If one partner incurs the debt, *all* the partners are still liable for its payment, even if this means selling personal possessions to pay off the debt of the business.

A partnership

Unless stated otherwise in the Deed of Partnership, the profits of the business are shared among the partners in proportion to the amount of capital each one invested in starting up the business. For example, if three partners each invested £10 000, they would each take equal shares from the profits; but if one partner had invested £15 000 and the two others had invested £7500, the first partner would receive 50 per cent of the profits and the other two partners would each receive 25 per cent.

 TALK IT OVER

Do you think it is fair that partners share profits equally, if they have each invested the same amount?

SETTING UP A PARTNERSHIP

When setting up a partnership the partners should draw up a Deed of Partnership. This could be a verbal agreement, however partners are advised to have a written document that states:

◆ the names of all the partners
◆ how much capital each is investing

◆ how the profits and losses will be shared among the partners
◆ the duties of each partner
◆ the procedures for admitting new partners and for partners leaving.

The **Partnership Act 1890** lays out the rules for setting up and running partnerships if a Deed of Partnership is not drawn up.

 TALK IT OVER
What might be included in a Deed of Partnership for a firm of architects?

ADVANTAGES

◆ A partnership is easy to set up.
◆ The amount of capital needed to start up the partnership is often small.
◆ Forming a partnership can mean that it is easier to raise extra capital when needed, as all the partners can contribute.
◆ Individual partners can specialise in certain areas.
◆ Within the partnership, partners have others with whom to share problems and talk over ideas.

DISADVANTAGES

◆ The partners have **unlimited liability** for the debts of the business.
◆ Profits must be shared between owners (whereas a sole trader can keep all of the profits).
◆ Decisions made by any *one* partner must be followed by *all* partners – even bad decisions!
◆ Partners disagree about the running of the business.
◆ If a partner dies or becomes bankrupt, the partnership must be dissolved.

 TALK IT OVER
Why do you think partnerships are suitable for professional services such as solicitors, accountants and dentists?

KEY POINTS

■ A **partnership** is when:
– more than one person owns the business
– the partners have unlimited liability.

■ A partnership:
– is usually a professional service, e.g. medicine or law
– needs a Deed of Partnership.

■ A **Deed of Partnership** details:
– who is part of the partnership
– how much capital each member put into the partnership
– how profits will be shared
– the duties of each partner
– how members can join or leave the partnership.

■ Advantages:
– easy to set up
– small amount of capital needed
– easier to raise capital
– can have a range of abilities.

■ Disadvantages:
– unlimited liability
– possible disagreement between partners
– partnership dissolved if any partner becomes bankrupt or dies
– profits are shared between partners.

Private limited companies

WHAT IS A PRIVATE LIMITED COMPANY?

A private limited company is often owned by people who know each other, such as family, friends or work associates. They buy shares in the company and become part-owners of the company. A 'share' is a part of the capital. Shares cannot be sold to the public or transferred without permission of all shareholders. This means that the owners can control who can buy shares – that is why it is called a *private* limited company.

To set up a private limited company there must be at least one shareholder, one director and one secretary, but there is no *upper* limit to the number of shareholders. A private limited company has Limited or Ltd at the end of its name, to distinguish it from a public limited company.

The shareholders have limited liability, which means that if the company has financial problems the shareholders can be held responsible only up to the value of their shares – they do not run the risk of having to sell their personal possessions to pay off debts. This is because the company has its own legal identity, separate from the shareholders. This also means that the company can sue and be sued.

Each year the company must hold an annual general meeting (AGM) of the shareholders. They also have to send an independently audited copy of the company accounts to the Registrar of Companies, and these accounts are available to the public.

SETTING UP A PRIVATE LIMITED COMPANY

Two documents need to be sent to the Registrar of Companies: the *Memorandum of Association* and the *Articles of Association*.

The Memorandum of Association gives details about the company such as:

Many private limited companies are owned by larger public limited companies (see Unit 1, Topic 9). Raleigh is an example: it is owned by Derby International Corporation

 TALK IT OVER

Why might an existing shareholder object to shares being sold to someone?

 TALK IT OVER

Why may several football clubs have started off as private limited companies?

River Island is a well-known private limited company

◆ the company's name
◆ the address of its registered office
◆ a statement of limited liability
◆ the amount of share capital to be raised
◆ the purpose of the company – that is, the main activity of the business.

The **Articles of Association** give details about how the company will be run, such as:

◆ rights of shareholders
◆ how directors will be appointed
◆ rules about meetings
◆ procedures to be followed at the annual general meeting.

When the Registrar of Companies is satisfied with all the details given in the two documents, he or she will issue a **Certificate of Incorporation** and the private limited company can then begin trading.

ADVANTAGES

◆ The shareholders have limited liability – if the company fails, they are liable for debts only up to the value of the amount they invested in shares. Their personal possessions are not at risk.
◆ The company can raise extra capital by selling more shares in the company, thus giving it a greater opportunity to expand.
◆ The shareholders can keep control of the business.
◆ The company can continue trading even if a shareholder dies, as this shareholder's shares can be transferred to someone else.
◆ The private limited company has its own legal status, separate from the shareholders. Like people, it can sue and be sued, and it can own property.

DISADVANTAGES

◆ Each year the accounts of the company must be audited – checked by independent accountants – and a copy sent to the Registrar of Companies: they are then available to the public.
◆ It is more difficult and more expensive to set up a limited company than a partnership or sole trader business.
◆ The private limited company cannot sell its shares on the Stock Market.

KEY POINTS

■ **Limited liability** – shareholders are responsible for debts up to the value of their shares.

■ A private limited company needs:
  – a **Memorandum of Association** and **Articles of Association**, to register the company with the **Registrar of Companies**
  – an **annual general meeting** (AGM) of shareholders
  – an **audited** set of **accounts**, available to the public: these are audited by independent accountants to check that they are honest and truthful.

■ A share is a part of the business's total capital. Shareholders are given **share certificates** showing how much of the capital they own.

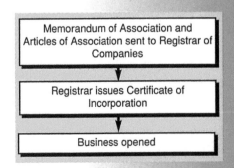

Memorandum of Association and Articles of Association sent to Registrar of Companies

↓

Registrar issues Certificate of Incorporation

↓

Business opened

WHAT IS A PUBLIC LIMITED COMPANY?

A public limited company has plc at the end of its name, distinguishing it from a private limited company.

Members of the general public, as well as other businesses and financial institutions, can buy shares in a public limited company. Most shares in public limited companies are owned by organisations rather than individuals. The shares of most UK public limited companies are bought and sold through the Stock Exchange. Share prices are printed in some of the national newspapers each day, so that the public can check on the current status of their shares.

The London Stock Exchange

The shareholders, as in the private limited company, have limited liability and can be held responsible only for payments up to the value of their shares. Like the private limited company, a public company has its own legal status separate from the shareholders. This also means that the company can sue and be sued.

Public limited companies often start as private limited companies. The private limited company may wish to grow, but it cannot offer its shares to the general public, so it may decide to 'go public'.

SETTING UP A PUBLIC LIMITED COMPANY

The procedure for setting up a public limited company is more complicated than that for a private limited company. The procedures are similar in that both a Memorandum of Association and Articles of Association must be sent to the Registrar of Companies, who will issue a Certificate of Incorporation when the public limited company shows that £50 000 capital can be raised. If the company is going to sell shares on the Stock Exchange it must be approved by the Stock Exchange Council. Once the Certificate of Incorporation has been issued the company can issue a prospectus – an advertisement inviting the public to buy shares in the company. When the shares have been issued the

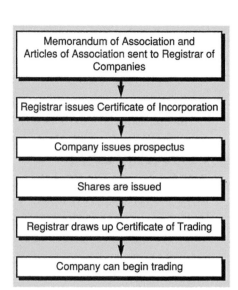

Memorandum of Association and Articles of Association sent to Registrar of Companies

↓

Registrar issues Certificate of Incorporation

↓

Company issues prospectus

↓

Shares are issued

↓

Registrar draws up Certificate of Trading

↓

Company can begin trading

Registrar of Companies will draw up a **Certificate of Trading**: this allows the company to start trading.

Instead of inviting the public to buy shares through the prospectus, a merchant bank could buy all the shares. The merchant bank would then advertise an **offer for sale** and the public would buy the shares from the bank. This approach would allow the merchant bank to keep the unsold shares and also to retain an interest in the company.

The public limited company must have at least two shareholders, two directors and a company secretary. There must be an **annual general meeting** for the shareholders, and accounts must be audited annually and a copy must be sent to the Registrar of Companies, this copy being available to the public.

ADVANTAGES

◆ The shareholders have limited liability.
◆ It is easy to raise capital for expansion by issuing more shares to the public.
◆ It is much easier to raise finance because the banks are much more willing to lend money to a large, well-established company, which they will see as a much smaller risk.

DISADVANTAGES

◆ It is expensive to set up, and at least £50 000 has to be raised.
◆ An **annual report** as well as **annual accounts** must be sent to all shareholders. These are also available for the general public and competitors to see.
◆ Anyone can buy shares, making the company vulnerable to **takeover** (Unit 4, Topic 10).

KEY POINTS

■ A public limited company needs:
– to be registered with the **Registrar of Companies**
– a prospectus to attract people to buy shares
– to hold an **annual general meeting** (AGM) of shareholders
– to make **audited accounts** available to the public.

■ Advantages:
– limited liability
– capital raised by selling shares
– easier to raise finance as seen as less of a risk.

■ Disadvantages:
– annual accounts and reports must be made public
– expensive to set up
– needs at least £50 000 in capital
– size of company can affect decision-making.

BUSINESS IN PRACTICE

Richard Branson started his business as a private limited company. Later, when the business had become very successful, Branson successfully floated the business on the Stock Exchange, and Virgin became a public limited company.

Not very long after becoming a plc, however,

Branson bought back all the shares and Virgin returned to being a private limited company.

 TALK IT OVER
Why do you think Branson did this?

TEST YOUR UNDERSTANDING

TOPICS 5–9

1 What is a *business objective*?

2 Explain why stakeholders in a business might not agree about business objectives.

3 What are the differences between a sole trader and a partnership?

4 Describe any advantages a sole trader has compared with a partnership.

5 Explain what *unlimited liability* means to a sole trader or a partner.

6 Why might an owner choose to form a private limited company rather than a partnership?

7 Describe the differences between a *private limited company* and a *public limited company*.

8 Discuss why limited liability encourages the sale of shares.

9 State the differences in procedure between forming a private limited company and a public limited company.

CASE STUDY

The Internet has opened up many opportunities for smaller businesses to compete with their bigger rivals. By promoting their skills through a well-designed website, these smaller businesses have greatly reduced previous marketing disadvantages.

The Committed Partnership is a design business that specialises in website design, Internet promotion and leaflet distribution for the UK tourist industry. The business is based in Cornwall but has customers all over the country. The partners believe that as tourism is one of Britain's most successful industries, it is essential that tourism-related activities are supported by an effective and efficient marketing strategy.

Clik is a graphic design consultancy. The partnership, which was established in 1993 in Canterbury, describes itself as 'multidisciplinary': it combines creative and management skills. Clik believes that it offers the same high standards as larger firms but in a more personal way, responding directly to the needs of the client.

1 What is the business activity of these two firms?

2 Describe the possible business objectives of each business.

3 Why might the owners have decided to form a partnership rather than any other form of business organisation?

4 Unlimited liability is one of the main disadvantages of a partnership. Explain why this might not be so important for the design partnerships.

5 Neither business wants to expand to any great extent. Discuss why the owners might feel like this.

22

EXAM PRACTICE

Greggs plc specialises in making and selling sandwiches, savouries, and other bakery products. John Gregg started this family business as a sole trader in the 1930s, when he opened the first shop with a small bakery at the back. Greggs still had only one shop in 1962.

John's son, Ian Gregg, took over as managing director in 1964. Since flotation in 1984, Greggs plc has developed into a major retailer, now owning 1100 shops all over the UK.

1 What is a sole trader?   [3 marks]

2 Suggest two business objectives John Gregg might have had when he started
the family business. Give reasons for your suggestions.   [6 marks]

3 Explain how Ian Gregg's business objectives were different from his father's.   [3 marks]

4 Discuss the advantages Ian Gregg hoped to gain when he converted Greggs
into a public company.   [8 marks]

Greggs plc is the UK's leading retailer specialising in sandwiches, savouries, and other bakery products, with a particular focus on takeaway food and catering. John Gregg started this family business in the 1930s, when he opened the first shop with a small bakery at the back. Greggs still had only one shop in 1962.

John's son, Ian Gregg, took over as managing director in 1964. Since flotation in 1984 Greggs plc has developed into a major retailer now owning 1100 shops all over the UK.

1 Discuss why Ian Gregg wanted Greggs to be a plc. Give reasons for your answer. [14 marks]

2 Suggest why Greggs is moving in the direction of takeaway food.   [6 marks]

TOPIC 10 Co-operatives

WHAT IS A CO-OPERATIVE?

A co-operative is an organisation which is owned and controlled by its members. The members of co-operatives aim to help each other and believe in social responsibility.

In addition to consumer co-operatives – which are the organisations that most people think of when co-operatives are mentioned – there are housing co-ops, worker co-ops and credit unions.

THE CO-OPERATIVE GROUP

The Co-operative Group is the largest consumer co-operative; in 2001 it comprised 44 consumer societies. In addition to consumer societies the group also owns the Co-operative Bank and the Co-operative Insurance Society (CIS). Co-operatives are the leaders in the UK funeral business and are also Britain's biggest farmer, working nearly 100 000 acres.

Retailing co-operatives are diverse, dealing in food, travel, the motor trade and chemist shops.

TALK IT OVER
If you owned a lot of shares, would you be happy with just one vote?

TALK IT OVER
Why do you think that the Co-operative Group is so diversified?

BUSINESS IN PRACTICE

The Co-operative Society was set up in 1844 in Rochdale in Lancashire. A group of workers, known as the Rochdale Pioneers, decided to buy food and other goods at wholesale prices and sell them cheaply to the members of the group. The profits from sales were then shared by the members in the form of a dividend. This was worked out from the amount of money the members spent – the more they spent the more they received back. This was the start of the Co-operative Retail Society (CRS).

TALK IT OVER
Would profits have been important to the Rochdale Pioneers?

PRINCIPLES OF CO-OPERATIVES

The key values of all co-operatives are the same.

◆ Membership is open and voluntary – anyone can join.

◆ Members are always in control – some co-ops have equal voting rights (one member, one vote) while others might have elected representatives.

◆ Members contribute to capital and control the use of capital, for example setting up reserves.

◆ Co-operatives are committed to education and training of their members and employees.

◆ Co-operatives are independent organisations which try to strengthen the co-operative movement by working together locally, nationally and internationally.

◆ Co-operatives are committed to promoting the development of communities.

 TALK IT OVER

Are these principles (agreed in 1996) the same as those of the Rochdale Pioneers?

BUSINESS IN PRACTICE

The 'Co-op' organisation in the UK today has changed considerably since 1844. Some smaller food retailing branches and furniture producers have disappeared while others have grown in strength – banking, travel, insurance, farming and funeral services.

The organisation prides itself on the contribution it makes to society. For example, the bank's investment in ethical projects only is well known, as is the organisation's contribution to education.

 TALK IT OVER

Are the principles of the Co-op organisation still the same as they were in 1844? Why might some of the retail branches have disappeared?

KEY POINTS

A business is a **co-operative** when:

■ it is owned by its members who might be consumers or workers

■ all members have a right to vote

■ members make decisions

■ each member has only one vote.

WHAT IS A FRANCHISE?

Franchising is an agreement in which one business, the franchisee, buys the right to sell the goods or services of another business, the franchisor, and is allowed to use the franchisor's name. There are many examples of franchising, including The Body Shop, McDonald's, KFC, Benetton, Thorntons, Burger King, Prontaprint and the British School of Motoring (BSM). The franchisee has an increased chance that their business will succeed, because of the established reputation and support of the franchisor.

SETTING UP A FRANCHISE

The franchisee must agree to run the business in the way required by the franchisor. This means that quality and standards are maintained. In return, the franchisor will:

- allow the franchisee to use the well-known brand name
- provide training to start the business
- provide equipment and shop fittings
- organise advertising campaigns, including a launch of the new business

Burger King and The Body Shop are examples of franchising

THE FRANCHISEE

Advantages	Disadvantages
Good chance of success because of the well-known name	The franchisee will never feel that the business is theirs – for example, the business cannot be sold without permission
Ready-made reputation because the franchisor controls the quality of all franchises	The franchisee cannot make many decisions, because all franchises must be run according to the rules of the franchisor
Sound financial advice, so cash-flow problems are avoided – most business failures are due to cash-flow problems	The franchise could be withdrawn at any time without any explanation or compensation
Ready source of advice and funding	Fees, royalties and expensive stock make franchising a costly way to run a business
The franchisor is responsible for costly activities such as market research and product development	Royalties must be paid even if the business makes a loss

THE FRANCHISOR

Advantages
The franchisor can expand quickly without the need for a lot of capital
The franchisor does not lose control of the business
The franchisee will be motivated to make the business a success
The franchisor receives fees and royalties from the franchisor
The franchisor does not have a large workforce to manage

 provide advice and loans when needed

 supply stock and materials.

The franchisee has to pay for these benefits by giving the franchisor a **start-up fee** for a licence. A **royalty** – a percentage of the turnover – is then paid annually to the franchisor.

 TALK IT OVER

Can you think of any disadvantage of franchising for the franchisor?

TALK IT OVER

Why is it important that all of the businesses with a given franchise look the same?

TALK IT OVER

About half of all new businesses fail, but only a very small number of these are franchises. Why might this be the case?

KEY POINTS

- **Franchise** – an agreement by one business to allow another business to sell its products or services.
- **Franchisor** – the business that sells the right to use its name to sell its products or services.
- **Franchisee** – the business that agrees to pay for a franchise.

BUSINESS IN PRACTICE

Lion Garages Ltd held a Rover franchise. Lion's market was protected to some extent by Rover controlling the number of franchises in the area. This gave Lion a monopoly in a 10-mile radius.

When Rover reviewed the retailing of their cars, many franchises were withdrawn from smaller garages. Lion Garages Ltd was one of the franchisees from which the franchise was withdrawn. Lion Garages Ltd now has a franchise for Proton cars.

 TALK IT OVER

Why do you think that Lion Garages Ltd entered another franchise agreement?

Globalisation is the term used to describe the development of world markets. Businesses are now looking to sell their products all over the world, rather than just in the UK or the US, and this has led to an increase in both the number and the size of multinational companies. Improved worldwide communications have made it easier to develop a global economy.

 TALK IT OVER

How many products can you think of that are the same all over the world?

MULTINATIONALS

A multinational company is simply a company that owns and controls other companies all over the world. Saying what *is* might be simple, but describing the organisation of a multinational is far from simple!

A multinational has a parent company which controls all other parts of the organisation. The parent company owns many subsidiary companies, which will be located all over the world. The parent company is a public company, and is usually the only shareholder of the subsidiary companies.

Coca Cola is a global product

TALK IT OVER

Why do most subsidiary companies have the parent company as the only or majority shareholder?

Multinationals generally set up production in additional countries in order to gain some advantage. For example, Nissan came to the UK because they wanted to break into the European market. Trade barriers controlled the number of imported cars, but cars were considered to be 'European' if a certain percentage of their parts were produced in Europe. By setting up production in the UK, Nissan could sell as many 'British' cars as they pleased.

Other reasons for setting up production in other countries include allowing the multinational to take advantage of low wages or to be sited close to raw materials.

KEY POINTS
- **Global economy** – the world as a single market.
- **Multinational** – a business that owns production units all over the world.
- **Parent company** – the company that owns and controls all parts of the organisation.
- **Subsidiary company** – the parts of the multinational controlled and owned by the parent company.

BUSINESS IN PRACTICE

Nestlé is one of the world's biggest multinationals. In 2000 it employed 224 000 people, producing 479 products in 81 countries. The product range is generally concerned with food, but has also diversified into pharmaceuticals; Nestlé is a world leader in optical products.

Nestlé UK Ltd is the subsidiary that controls business activity in the UK. It focuses on five product groups:

- beverages – coffee and milk drinks
- food – chilled meats, sauces, pasta, spreads and desserts
- Rowntree – sweets, chocolate and chocolate biscuits
- nutrition – nutritious snacks, drinks and supplements
- ice cream – ice cream and ice lollies.

Nestlé UK has a turnover of over £1600 million, of which exports total £200 million.

 TALK IT OVER

What kind of problems might a multinational like Nestlé come

The UK is a mixed economy – most businesses are privately owned, but some organisations that provide goods and services are run and owned by the state (see Topic 2). The two main sections of the public sector are:

- central government
- local government.

CENTRAL GOVERNMENT

Central government provides services to the public, either free or by charging a fee. We are all able to go to a doctor when we feel ill – the National Health Service provides doctors; the public pays for them with taxes such as income tax and VAT (Value Added Tax). Fees such as dental charges and prescription charges also help to pay for the National Health Service. Other public services include defence and the provision of main roads around the country.

LOCAL GOVERNMENT

Local government is run by local councils: they provide services such as education, police, fire services, social services, council housing, libraries and local roads.

A large percentage of the money for providing these services comes from central government, the rest from householders paying Council Tax and from taxes on local businesses paying National Non-Domestic Rates (Business Rate). National Non-Domestic Rates (Business Rate) are paid to cover the services provided to local businesses by the local authority, such as cleaning the streets and collecting refuse. National Non-Domestic Rates (Business Rate) are calculated as a percentage of the value of the building.

Some services provided by local government, such as leisure centres, are self-financing.

The government is responsible for the Post Office

BUSINESS IN PRACTICE

In 1994 Railtrack took over from British Rail, a nationalised industry. In December 1998 Railtrack was in dispute with the government's rail regulator. In March 1999 Railtrack's investment programme was criticised.

The government's rail regulator set up an investigation into Railtrack. The report criticised Railtrack for not investing enough of their profits of '£1 million a day' into the maintenance and renewal of tracks and signalling equipment.

Adapted from Paul Marston: 'Railtrack is condemned for declining track quality', *The Daily Telegraph*, 14.4.99

TALK IT OVER

Consider the derailments during 2000. Has privatising British Rail been a success?

PUBLIC CORPORATIONS

Public corporations are owned by the government – it is as if the government owned all the shares. A public corporation is set up by an Act of Parliament, and the government appoints a **board of directors** to be responsible for its running.

The government now is responsible for the British Broadcasting Corporation (BBC) and the Post Office. There used to be a large number of organisations in the public sector, including British Gas, British Rail, British Telecom, but most such organisations have now been privatised.

PRIVATISATION

In the 1980s and 1990s the majority of public corporations and nationalised industries in the public sector were sold into the private sector. The Conservative government at the time believed that competition would make them more efficient and profitable.

Most of these businesses were **monopolies**. To protect the interests of the consumers, **regulatory bodies** were set up. For example, Ofgas and Oftel were formed to make sure that the newly formed gas and telephone companies did not exploit the consumer.

THE PUBLIC AND PRIVATE SECTORS

It is easy to confuse public and private sectors. The main differences are given in the table below:

KEY POINTS

- The **public sector** comprises central government and local government.
- The public sector provides essential services that are not considered profitable, and protects industries seen as vital to the country's interests.
- Many nationalised industries were **privatised** to make them more efficient.
- A **monopoly** exists when one business can control a market.

 TALK IT OVER

Why might a private sector business not want to run a leisure

Public sector	Private sector
Owned by the government	Owned by private individuals – just like you!
Public sector organisations aim to provide essential services – e.g. Royal Mail	Private sector business aims to make profits and promote growth
Decisions are made by the board of directors **appointed** by the government	Decisions are made by the sole trader, the partners, or the board of directors **elected** by the shareholders
Finance comes from loans, government grants, and any surplus income the organisation might have	Finance comes from the owners and loans from financial institutions

Management structures

The management structure for an organisation describes the different levels of responsibility, and how decisions are put into practice. This structure can be represented by an organisation chart.

ORGANISATION CHARTS

An organisation chart shows the chain of command – the way in which decisions are passed up or down the organisation, from one level to the next – and the span of control – the number of employees for whom a person at a higher level has direct responsibility.

TALK IT OVER

Different structures are described here. What types of business might each structure suit?

TALL STRUCTURES

A tall organisation is one in which there is a long chain of command: as the chart shows, decisions pass through several levels of management. The span of control in a tall organisation chart is usually quite narrow.

This management structure is a hierarchy with several clear levels of responsibility. People on the same level of the chart have equal responsibility and each is directly responsible for their subordinates – the people immediately below them.

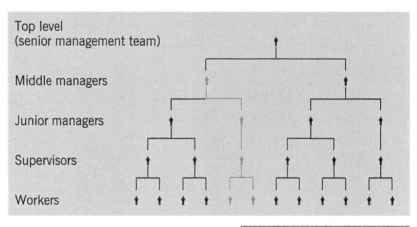

Top level
(senior management team)

Middle managers

Junior managers

Supervisors

Workers

Tall organisation:
long chain of command

Advantages	Disadvantages
A narrow span of control makes it easy for managers to monitor workers	The hierarchy is inflexible
The chain of command shows a clear line for communications	This can cause friction between workers at different levels
	Junior staff may feel remote and under-valued
	Decisions take longer to be put into action

FLAT STRUCTURES

A **flat organisation** has a short chain of command – decisions do not have to pass through many levels of management. In a flat organisation, the span of control is usually quite wide.

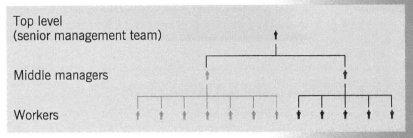

Flat organisation: wide span of control

People in lower levels tend to be given more responsibility. Managers need to be confident in their staff, and happy to delegate work to subordinates.

Advantages	Disadvantages
Fewer managers are needed, as workers have more responsibility	Managers are responsible for many people
Increased responsibility gives workers greater job satisfaction	Managers have to rely on subordinate staff to implement decisions
The shorter chain of command means more efficient decision-making	The wide span of control could cause the manager to lose control

BUSINESS IN PRACTICE

The Swan pub is owned and run by Mr and Mrs Swan! It is a small pub with a restaurant. There are also six chalets for overnight guests. Occasionally functions are organised, both for businesses and for the public. Mr and Mrs Swan are assisted by some full- and part-time employees.

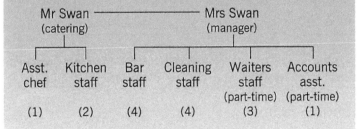

 TALK IT OVER

What problems could arise with this management structure?

KEY POINTS

■ Most businesses have a management structure that can be shown on an **organisation chart**.

■ The **chain of command** is the route by which decisions are passed between different levels of an organisation.

■ The **span of control** is the number of subordinates for whom a manager has direct responsibility.

■ **Delegation** means giving authority to subordinates to make certain decisions.

FUNCTIONAL ORGANISATION

There are different ways in which a business can be organised, but larger businesses tend to be organised by function. The diagram below is a **functional organisation chart**, showing the top levels of the organisation chart in a retail business. The business is structured according to the business *functions* – marketing, sales, purchasing, finance and human resources.

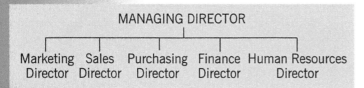

In a manufacturing business, a production (or operations) manager would be included.

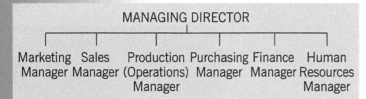

If the business operates throughout the country, or even throughout the world, it could be organised by *region*: McDonald's, for example, is organised by countries. A business based only in the UK, on the other hand, could be organised by regions.

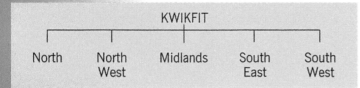

A business can also be organised by *product*, as in the case of Unilever.

CENTRALISATION

Many businesses are organised centrally. This means that major decisions are made by head office, and passed to regional managers around the country. The advantage of such **centralisation** is that all

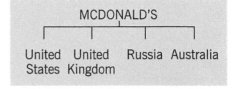

of the business are run to the same format, and there is tight central control of decision-making. The down-side of centralisation is that regional managers may not feel in control, head office may not understand regional differences, and decisions may be slow to be put into action.

DECENTRALISATION

Decentralisation means that, apart from those relating to major issues, decisions are delegated to regional managers. This motivates managers and encourages competition *within* the business. Regional managers can act quickly to make changes in their area. However, some managers may lack the necessary expertise, or may not understand the wider effect of their decisions on the business. Branches working independently will also lose some economies of scale.

 TALK IT OVER

Would centralisation be of benefit to a national chain of travel agents?

STAFF MANAGERS

Some businesses employ **staff managers**. These managers are experts in their subjects, for example computerised systems. Staff managers do not fit into a functional structure because they advise and support *all* departments. Human resources managers are sometimes considered to be staff managers.

KEY POINTS

■ **Functional structure** – departments organised according to function (what they do), region (where they are), or product (what they make).

■ **Line managers** have direct control over workers immediately below them in the organisation chart.

■ **Staff managers** are specialists who give support and advice to all line departments.

■ The **span of control** is the number of people on the level below a given manager, for whom that manager has direct responsibility.

■ **Decision-making** can be:
  – **centralised**: all major decisions are made by the directors, often based in a head office
  – **decentralised**: most decisions are made by managers in individual departments
  – **delegated**: particular individuals are given authority to make certain kinds of decision.

TEST YOUR UNDERSTANDING

TOPICS 10-15

1 What is a co-operative?
2 What are the differences between members of a co-operative and shareholders of a company?
3 Why is franchising a 'different way to start a business'?
4 Explain what is meant by *globalisation*.
5 Explain how a multinational might be organised.
6 What is the difference between local and central government?
7 What is a nationalised industry?
8 Why were many public sector organisations privatised?
9 Explain what is meant by *delegation*.
10 Explain the difference between a line manager and a staff manager.

CASE STUDY

McDonald's is a franchising organisation. If a business has a franchise with McDonald's, its owners will be able to run the restaurant for 20 years unless they break the terms of the agreement.

McDonald's give the franchisee the right to use their trademarks, signs, recipes, accounting systems and marketing strategies. This is so that the restaurant looks, and is run like, every other McDonald's restaurant.

The cost to the business owner is £250 000 or more for a franchise. The business owner must provide at least 25% of this fee from the owner's personally owned funds – this is £62 500. McDonalds will help the business owners who do not have this kind of money by offering a Business Facilities Lease (BFL); this is a kind of 'earn-in' scheme allowing a franchisee to use the profits from the business to buy the restaurant in the first three years of the franchise.

1 What is a franchise?
2 How would McDonald's help a new franchisee?

3 Why is a franchised business more likely to succeed than any other new start-up?
4 Why might the owner of a McDonald's restaurant be less satisfied than someone who started his or her own business?
5 Explain why McDonald's marketing strategies would be an advantage to a new business.

EXAM PRACTICE

◆ Gems Ltd is a chain of jewellers with shops and workshops throughout the country. As well as selling a wide range of jewellery, Gems is famous for producing handmade jewellery. The shops in bigger towns and cities also carry collectable china.

All decisions are made at head office, with branch managers having very little authority. For example, head office decides about advertising, window displays, recruitment, accounting systems, customer service and even staff holiday rotas. Gems is organised as a hierarchy.

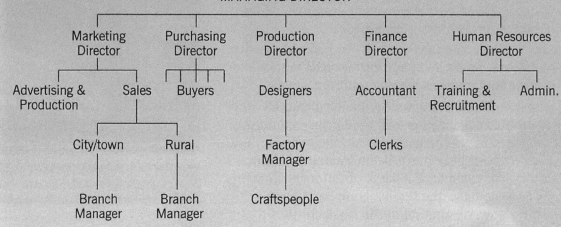

1 Describe the chain of command in Gems. [3 marks]

2 Describe the span of control in Gems. [3 marks]

3 Describe two problems that could arise from Gems' organisational structure. Give reasons for your suggestions. [6 marks]

4 Explain how Gems' management could solve one of the problems you identified in **3**. [4 marks]

5 Discuss the advantages of Gems' organisation becoming more decentralised. [4 marks]

◆ Gems Ltd is a chain of jewellers with shops and workshops throughout the country. As well as selling a wide range of jewellery, Gems is famous for producing handmade jewellery. The shops in bigger towns and cities also carry collectable china.

All decisions are made at head office, with branch managers having very little authority. For example, head office decides about advertising, window displays, recruitment, accounting systems, customer service and even staff holiday rotas. Gems is organised as a hierarchy.

1 Identify any problems that could arise from Gems' organisational structure, and suggest how these problems could be solved. [8 marks]

2 The Gems chain is organised by function. It could alternatively be organised by region or by product. Explain, giving reasons, how you would organise the business if you were the managing director. [6 marks]

3 'Gems would be better managed if the decision making was decentralised.' Explain why the managing director might believe this to be true. [6 marks]

LOCAL GOVERNMENT

The local government can offer advice and information to businesses on matters such as:

- how to obtain **grants** from the European Union and central government
- **planning permission** for new premises
- planning permission for existing premises, where a change of business is proposed
- how to find a suitable location – to help prospective businesses, many local authorities keep **registers** of land and premises for sale and rent locally.

Planning permission is given by the local council only if it is felt that the business will benefit the community. Before planning permission is given, the business may be asked to contribute towards improving the local amenities. For example, if a large out-of-town shopping centre is to be built, the retailers may be asked to contribute towards upgrading the roads in the immediate area, to cope with the increase in traffic that will occur. For many areas with high unemployment, the local government will be mainly concerned with attracting new businesses to provide jobs.

Large out-of-town shopping centres need planning permission

 TALK IT OVER

How has any new business affected the area where you live?

LOCAL ENVIRONMENT

When a large business starts up in a new area it may have a number of influences on the local people and environment:

- it creates jobs
- it may create work for other local businesses, such as local shops near to the new business
- it puts money into the local economy by paying business rates to the local council and wages to local workers
- it may contribute to the local infrastructure, by building new roads or a school near the business

 TALK IT OVER

Discuss the view that it is easier to gain planning permission in areas of high unemployment.

◆ it will train new employees
◆ it can provide a more skilled workforce for the local community.

However, the new business might:

◆ create pollution
◆ put a strain on local facilities such as roads and services such as the police.

These are known as **social costs** and **social benefits**.

SOCIAL COSTS

Social costs include:

◆ damage to animals and plants
◆ strains on the local infrastructure, such as overcrowding in schools and hospitals
◆ increased congestion on roads
◆ increased air and noise pollution.

SOCIAL BENEFITS

Social benefits include:

◆ creating jobs for suppliers and local businesses, such as local shops and restaurants.

It will also have national effects – the business has to pay corporation tax, and the employees have to pay income tax and national insurance, all of which contribute to the national economy.

 TALK IT OVER

What are the social costs and social benefits of a local business?

KEY POINTS

■ **Social costs** – the negative effects a business has on the community.

■ **Social benefits** – the positive effects a business has on the community.

Planning new local development

BUSINESS IN PRACTICE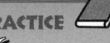

Nestlé has the following aims:

• to create jobs
• to buy local raw materials
• to work with the local community
• to provide training and advice
• to pursue scientific development.

TALK IT OVER

Will the local authority consider all these aims to be social benefits?

Central government influence

Central government has great influence on business.

ECONOMIC POLICY

Each government, of whichever political party, has economic policies to achieve its objectives. These objectives might be, for instance, to reduce unemployment, to improve the National Health Service, and to control inflation.

Different economic policies are used for different objectives. For example, the government might *encourage* consumer spending in order to reduce unemployment, or *discourage* consumer spending in order to counteract rising inflation.

INFLATION

The term inflation means a sustained increase in the general level of prices. Inflation is usually described as a sustained percentage rise in the general price level.

The government always tries to keep the rate of inflation *low*. If the rate of inflation rises, the cost of raw materials and transport will both rise: businesses will have to increase the price of their goods to pay for these increases. Workers will want a pay rise, to keep up with the increase in their cost of living and the higher prices they now have to pay. Businesses can lose as the consumer may not be able to buy so much because of this increase in prices.

TAXES

The government can use changes in the rates of taxes and duties as part of its economic policies. Changes in these will influence businesses. The main taxes used by the government are these:

◆ Income tax is charged at different rates on people's income from their work, their pension, or the interest on their bank or building society account.

Mortgage shock – rates up again

Bank of England warns of more interest rises

Inflation up to $3\frac{1}{2}\%$

 TALK IT OVER

Why does nobody benefit from inflation?

- **Corporation tax** is paid by companies on their profits.
- **Value Added Tax (VAT)** is paid on most goods and services bought, except essential items such as food and children's clothing.
- **Customs duties** are charged on some goods imported into this country.
- **Excise duties** are charged on goods such as petrol, beer, wine, spirits and cigarettes.

If the government lowers the rate of tax, the consumer will have more money to spend: this means that there will be a greater demand for goods and services, which in turn will mean there will have to be an increase in supply. As a result, businesses should see an increase in profits.

INTEREST RATES

Interest rates are the rates charged for borrowing money over a set period of time. Most businesses at some time have to borrow money from financial institutions. There are several different rates of interest, from different institutions and for different types of loan.

If the rate of interest is *increased*, more money than originally expected will need to be repaid for borrowing the money: therefore the loan will become more expensive. If the interest rate *falls*, less interest will need to be paid: therefore the loan will become cheaper.

High interest rates deter both businesses and consumers from borrowing money. High interest rates may also encourage people to save their money rather than spend it. This has a knock-on effect on businesses, as demand for goods and services falls.

If the **Bank of England** considers that low interest rates are encouraging inflation, then interest rates will increase.

LAWS

The government has introduced a range of legislation that directly influences business. The Sex Discrimination and Race Relations Acts were introduced to provide **equal opportunities**; and other legislation covers **health and safety** at work and **contracts of employment**. For more detail on employment laws, see Unit 3, Topic 6.

KEY POINTS

- Central government can influence business by:
  - changing taxation
  - changing public spending
  - influencing changes in interest rates.
- **Income tax** – money paid out of the wages, salaries and all other income of British citizens.
- **Corporation tax** – a percentage of a company's profits.
- **Rate of inflation** – the rate at which the price level rises.
- Central government also influences business by passing laws concerning:
  - equal opportunities
  - conditions of employment
  - health and safety at work.

TALK IT OVER

What would be the impact of high interest rates on an economy?

INFLUENCE OF PRESSURE GROUPS

A pressure group is a group of people who try to influence decisions made by businesses, government and consumers on a specific issue. Such groups have no political power, but seek to put their opinions across through activities such as demonstrations, seeking publicity, and lobbying Members of Parliament.

Pressure groups that try to protect the consumer and the environment may have great influence on businesses. For example, if local residents feel that the building of an out-of-town shopping centre near to their homes would affect their quality of life, through added noise levels or traffic pollution, they might form a pressure group to try to influence the council's decision about whether or not to give planning permission. Groups like these normally exist to protest only against one particular development.

Pressure groups express their opinions through demonstrations and publicity

 **TALK IT OVER**

What form might this protest take?

ENVIRONMENTAL ISSUES

Many well-known pressure groups, including Greenpeace and Friends of the Earth, exist to fight over a wide range of related issues throughout the world. These pressure groups can carry a great deal of influence over companies and governments, and often have support from the general public.

For example, when Shell tried to dump the Brent Spa oil platform at sea, Greenpeace launched a high-profile publicity campaign to stop them, claiming that to do so would damage the environment. Brent Spa is now in a Norwegian fiord and is likely to be dismantled and recycled, at a cost of around £16 million. Shell obviously thinks that this is worthwhile in order to preserve its image as a caring company.

 TALK IT OVER

Are pressure groups like these always 'good guys'?

CONSUMER RIGHTS

The Consumers' Association is another well-known pressure group: it tests products on the consumer's behalf, and publishes the results in its magazine, *Which?*

Television programmes such as *Watchdog* are now very popular: they also campaign for consumer rights against companies that they feel are not serving the consumers' best interests.

 TALK IT OVER

Do you know of any interesting consumer rights problems that have been solved?

 BUSINESS IN PRACTICE

Mothers are so concerned about the health hazards associated with mobile phones that they have formed protest groups all over the North East. They complain that mobile phones should not be promoted to children, and that masts are too close to schools, nurseries and retirement homes.

MP Peter Atkinson is concerned that loopholes in the law allow smaller masts to be erected without planning permission.

The possibility of an anti-Orange day is likely to target Orange's offices at Darlington.

Adapted from Graeme Whitfield: *The Journal*
(www.the-journal.co.uk), 30.1.01

 TALK IT OVER

How could Orange deal with these protests?

KEY POINTS

■ **Pressure groups** can be:
- local groups formed for one specific cause
- large international groups that have a range of interests and influence with governments and businesses.

■ Well-known pressure groups include:
- Greenpeace
- Friends of the Earth
- the Consumers' Association.

International influences

EXPORTS AND IMPORTS

Most businesses are likely to be affected by the international environment. A company may decide to export its goods to foreign countries in order to increase its sales; it will also hope to increase its market share. When buying raw materials, components, tools or equipment for the running of the business, the company will want to buy quality products at the lowest price: this may lead it to decide to **import** the goods from foreign countries if it can get better or cheaper supplies than from British suppliers.

A well-known British export

Exports are goods (also known as **trade in goods**) and services (also known as **trade in services**) that are made in this country and sold to foreign countries. Imports are goods and services that are made in foreign countries and brought into this country.

The Balance of Payments is a record of the *overall* results of the UK's trading activity with the rest of the world. It includes imports being bought and brought into this country and exports being sold and sent out of the country, as well as the capital flowing between the UK and other countries.

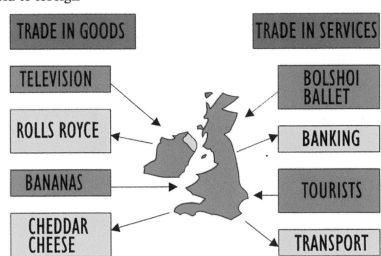

TRADE IN GOODS

TELEVISION

ROLLS ROYCE

BANANAS

CHEDDAR CHEESE

TRADE IN SERVICES

BOLSHOI BALLET

BANKING

TOURISTS

TRANSPORT

EXCHANGE RATES

The exchange rate states what the £ sterling is equal to in other currencies, for example *£1 = 250 pesetas* or *£1 = 10 French francs*. When the £ sterling becomes stronger, more foreign currency is needed to buy £1, for example *£1 = 275 pesetas* or *£1 = 12 French francs*.

European trade uses the **euro**, so the pound is valued against the euro. A 'strong' £ sterling makes British exports more expensive to other countries, and thus more difficult to sell. On the other hand, a 'weak' £ sterling is good for businesses' exports – their goods and services will be cheaper, and demand will increase.

 TALK IT OVER

Why is a strong £ good for British holiday tour operators?

COMPETING WITH FOREIGN BUSINESSES

The government can help businesses to compete with foreign companies in several ways:

◆ It can put **tariffs** on imports. This means that the government adds a tax to the price of goods made abroad but sold in this country. This may make the imported goods more expensive to buy than UK goods.

◆ It can **subsidise** exports. This means that the government gives the business a grant that allows it to lower the prices to be charged abroad. This is intended to encourage more sales.

◆ It can impose **quotas** on imports. This means that the government restricts the number of goods coming from foreign countries into the UK over the period of a year.

◆ It can try to influence the **value of the pound** so that imports are more expensive and UK goods are cheaper for foreign countries to buy.

In reality the government may be unable to help. The UK is a member both of the **European Union (EU)** and of the **World Trade Organisation (WTO)**. The EU does not allow tariffs and quotas on trade between member countries. The WTO puts controls on tariffs and quotas.

The EU is having more and more impact on UK businesses. All businesses in the European Union have to follow EU regulations, including health and safety regulations, employment regulations, and standards set for goods and services.

KEY POINTS

- **Exports** – businesses selling their products outside the country in which they are based.

- **Imports** – businesses buying products produced outside their country.

- Central government can help businesses to compete with foreign companies by:
  - subsidising exports
  - imposing tariffs on imports
  - imposing quotas on imports
  - influencing the exchange rate.

 TALK IT OVER

Should the government help British businesses to export goods?

BUSINESS IN PRACTICE

John Monks, General Secretary of the TUC, is concerned that the £ sterling is overvalued 30% against the euro. 'Many industries have modernised and their workforces have high rates of productivity but they are losing their competitiveness.'

The strength of sterling against the euro has been blamed for job losses by a number of firms including Ford and BMW.

The government refuses to threaten economic stability (inflation) for the sake of a lower exchange rate.

Adapted from George Jones: 'Blair refuses pleas to devalue pound', *The Daily Telegraph*, 15.5.00

 TALK IT OVER

Do you think that the government is right to stand its ground?

TEST YOUR UNDERSTANDING

1 Describe how local government can try to attract new businesses to set up in its area.
2 List three advantages to a local community of a large chemical firm being set up in the area.
3 Suggest why a business that wants to build extend premises might be refused planning permission by the local council.
4 What is a pressure group?
5 How can a pressure group try to change or influence decisions?
6 What is inflation?
7 Explain how inflation would affect your pocket money.
8 Describe how a shareholder might feel if corporation tax were increased.
9 Explain the difference between an import and an export.
10 How can the government help a UK business to increase its exports?

CASE STUDY

Trafford describes itself as 'an historic country home with deer roaming free, unequalled industrial heritage and archaeological sites, excellent shopping and the very best in sport and leisure'.

Trafford is mainly urban, and experts regularly monitor the environment for pollution. Much of this has been reduced by partnerships with industry.

Visitors can reach Trafford easily because it is on the doorstep of Manchester International Airport and in the centre of one of Britain's finest motorway and rail networks. Trafford also has the 'supertram' on the Metrolink connecting many local towns and villages.

The local authority is keen to promote sport and leisure. It has seven public leisure centres, offering a wide range of both indoor and outdoor activities with relaxing lounge/bar areas and restaurant facilities. In one leisure centre the maximum price charged for an activity is £4.20 and some activities such as swimming are as cheap as 90p.

1 Why does Trafford go to the expense of promoting the area?
2 How has Trafford reduced the levels of pollution in the area?
3 Explain why transport is an important aspect of local government.
4 Why might the local authority be 'keen to promote sport and leisure'?
5 Would the prices for leisure facilities be the same if a private sector business owned the leisure centre? Give reasons for your answer.

EXAM PRACTICE

In September 2000 the UK experienced a near-shortage of petrol. This was because farmers and lorry drivers organised blockades of refineries in protest against the increase in petrol prices.

1 The farmers and the lorry drivers are pressure groups.
   What is a pressure group?   [2 marks]

2 Describe the methods of protest a pressure group might use.   [4 marks]

3 Explain the possible effect on farmers and lorry drivers of an
   increase in the price of petrol.   [4 marks]

4 Identify two other pressure groups. State their objectives.   [4 marks]

5 What did the farmers and lorry drivers hope to achieve?   [3 marks]

6 Why might the government ignore the protest made by
   the farmers and lorry drivers?   [3 marks]

1 Suggest reasons why the price of petrol might have risen.   [3 marks]

2 'Farmers and lorry drivers are pressure groups.' Explain what
   this statement means.   [3 marks]

3 Explain the possible consequences for farmers and lorry drivers
   of a rise in petrol prices.   [6 marks]

4 Discuss why the government and the pressure groups might not
   see the rise in petrol prices in the same way.   [8 marks]

TOPIC 1 What is marketing?

Marketing is 'the management process responsible for identifying, anticipating and satisfying consumers' requirements profitably' (from the Chartered Institute of Marketing).

Other definitions of marketing include:

'Marketing is about creating customers by looking at all your activities through their eyes and giving the customers what they want and at a profit.'

'Marketing is not just selling, it is about what a company believes about its products, it is about objectives and goals, it is the driving force for all the people who work there.'

From these definitions we can see that marketing activities include:

carrying out **market research** to identify customer needs and wants

producing a **product** that meets customer needs and wants

calculating the **price** that meets customer demand

producing the right **quantities** to supply customer demand

promoting the product to the customer

distributing the product to the **place** where it is convenient for the customer to buy it.

Marketing is important to the whole business. Without it, the business could find itself trying to sell a new product that few people want. This sort of mistake can lead to big financial losses, because the business will have spent a lot of money developing and setting up the new product, and promoting its launch. If a business cannot meet a customer's needs, the customer will go elsewhere. This could mean a drop in sales and in **market share** for the business.

Source: English Riviera Tourist Board

Promoting a product

Doing market research

This is the latest, most efficient freezer in the range and its a real bargain

Good market research should identify the customer's needs

MARKETING OBJECTIVES

The main objectives or targets of any marketing department in a business are:

- ◆ to look continually at the business's current market, and to be aware of things happening outside the business. For example, if your business makes washing-up liquid and there is a large rise in the sale of automatic dishwashers, this would be important for your market
- ◆ to find out consumer needs and wants by carrying out market-research activities
- ◆ to try to increase the business's sales and market share.

These objectives can only be achieved by the business if it is always trying to make sure that it is selling the right product, at the right price, in the right place, and promoting it in the right way at the right time. These are called the 4Ps (see Unit 2, Topic 4, for more information).

One example of a business that has changed its marketing mix to meet consumer demands is Alton Towers.

KEY POINTS

■ **Marketing** is used:
- to get current information about customers
- to predict future trends
- to produce the right products
- to increase sales.

■ A **marketing department**:
- looks at the current market
- finds out customer needs
- increases market share.

BUSINESS IN PRACTICE

In recent years, Alton Towers has made changes to its theme park, and market research shows that many more families now visit Alton Towers. Before, the marketing had been targeted mainly at the late teens and early twenties, with rides such as 'Nemesis' and 'The Corkscrew' being the main attractions. The management decided to invest money in the introduction of a range of new rides and attractions that particularly appealed to families, including 'Old Macdonald's Tractor Ride', 'Toyland Tours' and the 'Doodle-doo Derby', all of which are targeted specifically at young children.

As a result of this investment in new product development, and new promotion and marketing strategies, Alton Towers has seen an increase in visitors, and thus an increase in revenue.

 TALK IT OVER

Why is it important for Alton Towers to increase its market share?

WHAT IS A MARKET SEGMENT?

If a business sells its products to a wide range of people – its market – it may divide these people into smaller groups called segments. This allows the business to make different products to meet the different specific needs of each group. The market segment at which a business aims is called its target market. If a business manages to satisfy more people's needs, sales and market share may increase.

BUSINESS IN PRACTICE

Raleigh Industries makes bicycles. Forty years ago, you could buy a man's bicycle, a woman's bicycle, or a junior bicycle. Then the firms that make bicycles, including Raleigh, found out that people wanted to do different things with their bicycles. For example:

- some wanted to ride a bicycle to work
- some wanted a bicycle purely for leisure
- some wanted a bicycle for road use or racing
- some wanted a bicycle that could be used anywhere.

The idea developed of making different bicycles to meet different customers' needs: the market was broken down into segments.

Raleigh's market segment includes:

- tricycles for toddlers
- play bikes for 3–7-year-olds
- action bikes for the teenage market
- full-suspension off-road bicycles for mountain bikers
- racing bicycles for professional cyclists.

HOW ARE MARKETS SEGMENTED?

The market may be segmented in a variety of ways:

- Age – Raleigh can segment by age, producing a range of bicycles for toddlers, children, teenagers, and adults.
- Gender – Women's and men's bicycles have different designs.
- Socio-economic grouping – This segments the population according to social status and

TALK IT OVER

What are the different market segments among people who may visit travel agents?

TALK IT OVER

McDonald's offer a limited range of burgers to everyone on a global scale. How do you think the business has managed to mass-market itself so successfully?

Social grade	Social status	Head of household's occupation	Approximate % of total UK population
A	Upper middle class	Managerial, professional and administrative jobs such as solicitors, doctors, company directors	3.5
B	Middle class	Middle managers such as department managers, teachers	12–13
C1	Lower middle class	Supervisory or clerical workers such as junior managers and foremen	22
C2	Skilled working class	Skilled manual workers such as electricians, plumbers	32–33
D	Working class	Semi-skilled and unskilled workers such as production line workers, cleaners	19–20
E	Poorest in society	Long-term unemployed, casual workers, state pensioners	10

Source: Institute of Practitioners in Advertising

occupation. People in the higher grades are more likely to be able to afford a full-suspension off-road mountain bike.

◆ **Geography** – People who live in a built-up area are more likely to want a road bike; those in a rural area are more likely to want an off-road bicycle.

The table above shows the different socio-economic groupings. The table shows that households can be divided broadly into six different categories. Each category is organised according to the occupation of the **head of the household**. These socio-economic groupings are one of the most important ways used to divide up the market, as they reflect consumers' lifestyles and likely levels of disposable income.

KEY POINTS

■ **Market segment** – a group of people in a market, which may be based on age, gender, socio-economic grouping, or geography.

BUSINESS IN PRACTICE

Wall's ice cream is a well-recognised brand name. Under the umbrella of Wall's you would probably recognise other brand names such as Calippo, Solero, Magnum and Carte d'Or. All of these products are kinds of ice cream and all are produced by Wall's, but each is aimed at a particular market segment.

Magnum was the first ice cream developed for adults. Its advertising and promotion suggest luxury and indulgence. Calippo is aimed at a younger market. It is priced more cheaply and does not use such strong advertising.

Websites: www.walls.sg; www.unilever.com

TALK IT OVER

Why does Wall's have such a large range of products? Why not offer just one type of ice cream to everybody?

NICHE MARKET

A niche market is a small section of a market segment. It consists of a small group of consumers whose wants and needs can be clearly identified.

Small businesses often survive by providing goods and services to such groups of customers when their needs are not being met by the products of larger companies. Claire's Accessories, The Sock Shop and Marlow Foods Ltd (makers of Quorn) are all examples of businesses that provide products for niche markets.

Larger businesses, such as Raleigh, also produce products for niche markets, in this case to gain a greater market share.

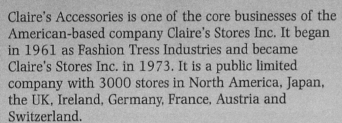

A bicycle manufacturer would produce a number of different types of bicycles for different markets, for example tricycles for toddlers and action bikes for teenagers. It might also produce bicycles for a niche market, for example made-to-measure bikes for professional racers.

BUSINESS IN PRACTICE

Claire's Accessories is one of the core businesses of the American-based company Claire's Stores Inc. It began in 1961 as Fashion Tress Industries and became Claire's Stores Inc. in 1973. It is a public limited company with 3000 stores in North America, Japan, the UK, Ireland, Germany, France, Austria and Switzerland.

Claire's Accessories is a retailer of room accessories (candles and photo frames), jewellery, stationery and cosmetics. The image is fun and bright – the colours pink, purple and red are popular.

The market segment at which Claire's aims its products is pre-teen and teenage females. The products are priced so that these customers can afford them.

Claire's uses teenage magazines for advertising and promotion. The marketing team try to create energy and excitement by using bright colours and links to popular bands. There is also a 'Claire's teen website' with information and advice on hosting parties, ear-piercing and Claire's products, and competitions.

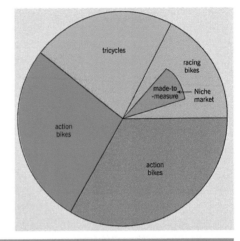

TALK IT OVER

Claire's Accessories caters for a niche market. What is it?

Identify the ways in which Claire's Accessories has met the wants and needs of its market segment.

BUSINESS IN PRACTICE

Holland & Barrett is the UK's largest health-food retailer. In early 2001 there were 426 stores, located throughout the UK, and many new stores were planned. You may recognise the green shop front in a town or city near you.

There has been a large increase in interest in natural food supplements over the last fifteen years or so. Holland & Barrett has grown with this increase in demand.

Holland & Barrett has almost eighty years of experience. Its scientists carry out research into natural food supplements that can improve our health and well-being. Ingredients from all over the world are used in more than a thousand different products, from aromatherapy oils to sports drinks. You can even buy vitamins for pets!

Holland & Barrett aims to give customers both value for money and quality. It trains its staff to give customers proper advice on all of the products and it regularly carries out checks on quality.

Holland & Barrett produces a magazine for its customers and holds the VMA (Vitamin Manufacturer of the Year Award).

Website: www.hollandbarrett.com
© Holland and Barrett Retail Limited 2001

 TALK IT OVER

Holland & Barrett has been successful in growing partly because its niche market has grown. What risks are faced by a business entering a niche market?

KEY POINTS

■ **Niche market** – a small, specific part of a market segment.

MARKETING MIX

In marketing a new product, the
business must put together the
right combination:

- the right product
- at the right price
- in the right place
- using the best method
  to promote the product
  to meet the wants and
  needs of the target market.

These factors – *product*, *price*,
place and *promotion* – are
often called the 4Ps.

Different goods and
services need appropriate
emphases for each of the
4Ps. For example, British Home
Stores uses mail shots to promote its
goods, but does not advertise on television: it puts
much more emphasis on producing high-quality
goods and selling them at reasonable prices – right
product, right price. Soft-drink manufacturers spend
a lot of money on promotion – advertising on
television and designing attractive packaging for
their goods. They also make sure that you can find
their brand of soft drink on the shelves of the local
supermarket – the right place.

The specific combination of the 4Ps chosen to suit
a particular product is called the marketing mix.

CHOOSING THE MIX

In choosing the mix, a business must consider the 4Ps.

Product

The business must have a product that customers
want, and for which they are prepared to pay. The
business may want to emphasise that the product is
of a high quality, that it has particular design
features, that it offers value for money, or perhaps
that it will improve the consumer's own image.

Packaging helps sell the product

Price

The business needs to know how much the customer is prepared to pay for the product, and what any competitors charge. The price must also be one that enables the business to make a profit. (You can read more about pricing methods in Unit 2, Topic 14.)

Place

The business needs to make sure that the product is being sold in the right type of **retail outlet**. For Raleigh, for example, this could be a specialist shop, such as a bicycle shop, or a large hypermarket that sells a wide range of goods, including bicycles. The decision is made by working out which type of outlet the target customer will visit, and placing the product there.

Some manufacturers are increasingly choosing **mail order** and the **Internet** to sell their products. Busy people often do not have the time to go to the shops; when buying goods they may prefer to browse through **catalogues** or surf the Net in the comfort of their own homes.

Promotion

The business needs to make sure that the customer *knows* about the new product and is encouraged to buy it. To inform the customer about products, businesses can use a range of methods, from word of mouth to expensive advertising campaigns. To encourage the customer to *buy* the product, the business may offer a **free gift** or a '**buy one, get one free**' (**BOGOF**) deal.

GETTING THE MIX RIGHT

To attract the target market, the marketing mix must be right. Businesses hope that by getting the marketing mix right they will have a **competitive edge** over their rivals. Large companies will often employ specialist firms such as **market research agencies** and **advertising agencies** to help them put together the right marketing mix.

The various measures taken by a business to satisfy customer needs are together known as its **marketing strategy**.

KEY POINTS

- The **4Ps** of the **marketing mix** are:
  – product
  – price
  – place
  – promotion.
- **Marketing strategy** – all the measures taken by a business to satisfy customer needs.

Some companies are now choosing the Internet to sell their products

 TALK IT OVER

Choose a product and describe its marketing mix.

Marketing is all about identifying consumer needs and wants, and developing a product to meet those needs and wants. Selling and promotion are about persuading consumers that they need or want to buy *your* product.

However, the consumer has to be protected against businesses that try to promote and sell their products through misleading or dishonest claims and descriptions of their products. As a result, measures have been introduced to protect the consumer, ranging from legal protection to voluntary codes of practice.

LEGAL PROTECTION

There are many laws that apply specifically to the ways in which businesses promote and sell their goods. Below are some of the most important ones.

The Trade Descriptions Act 1968 makes it an offence to describe goods falsely. For example, it is illegal to say that a garment is pure wool when it contains 20 per cent man-made fibres.

The Sale of Goods Act 1979 makes it an offence to sell goods that have defects. Goods must be of 'merchantable quality' (which means that they must be free from faults), 'fit for the purpose' for which they were made, and 'as described'.

The Consumer Protection Act 1987 makes it an offence to sell any *unsafe* goods, which might endanger life or cause injury, or which could cause damage to property. For example, some toys have been found to have buttons that could come off easily and on which a child could choke.

The Weights and Measures Act 1951 makes it an offence to sell short quantities. For example, to sell a packet of crisps that should weigh 25 g when it actually only weighs 15 g would break the law.

The Food Safety Act 1990 gives Environmental Health Officers the power to close down businesses where food is not being prepared hygienically.

The Consumer Credit Act 1974 states that businesses must state the true **annual**

percentage rate (APR) of interest being charged to customers who buy goods on credit. Customers must also have a period of time in which to change their minds after signing hire purchase contracts at home.

 TALK IT OVER

Give examples of ways that a business might break each of these laws.

HELP AND ADVICE FOR CONSUMERS

If consumers feel they need advice on consumer legislation, help may be found from a number of official and unofficial bodies set up to protect consumers.

The Office of Fair Trading (OFT) has wide-ranging powers to investigate complaints about misleading descriptions and prices, inaccurate weights and measures, consumer credit problems, and safety of goods. If the OFT feels that any business is working against the consumers' interests, it has the power to ban that business's goods or services.

The Consumers' Association tests a wide range of goods and services. It publishes the magazine *Which?*, in which it reports on investigations and tests it has carried out on the consumer's behalf. Other unofficial bodies that exist to protect consumer rights include the BBC's *Watchdog* series of programmes, the Citizens Advice Bureaux, and Consumer Advice Centres.

 TALK IT OVER

What does each of these symbols tell the customer about the product?

CERTIFICATION TRADE MARK
PURE NEW WOOL

VOLUNTARY CODES OF PRACTICE

As well as laws protecting the consumer, there are other constraints on the way organisations behave that have implications for marketing. Several industries and associations have voluntary codes of practice which their members are expected to follow. For example, the Press Association has a code of practice governing newspapers; and travel agents have their own code of practice which is monitored by ABTA (the Association of British Travel Agents).

One of the most successful voluntary codes of practice applies to advertising. The British Codes of Advertising and Sales Promotion were drawn up in 1962 to monitor all printed and cinema advertising. The codes state that all advertisements must be 'legal, decent, honest and truthful'. The Advertising Standards Authority (ASA) is responsible for supervising the British Codes of Advertising and Sales Promotion. If the ASA considers that in a particular advertisement an advertising company has not kept to the standards agreed, it can ask all newspapers, magazines and cinemas to refuse to display that advertisement. This code of practice does not apply to radio or television advertising but the ASA does regulate electronic advertising, for instance on the Internet, mobile phone messaging, on CDs and videos.

The Independent Television Commission (ITC) was set up in 1990 to control television advertising.

PRESSURE GROUPS

Pressure groups can also put constraints on businesses. In recent years, several companies have been forced by public demand to change their advertising methods.

A series of Benetton advertisements met with strong public disapproval and were eventually withdrawn. The government has put pressure on cigarette companies by banning cigarette advertising on television. It has now taken this ban one stage further, banning cigarette companies from advertising their sponsorship of major sporting events such as

The Body Shop led the campaign to ban cosmetic testing on animals

the World Snooker Championships.

Other areas of marketing that have been affected by public pressure are:

◆ The use of animals in testing for medicines and cosmetics. Many businesses now feel that it is important to declare that they do *not* use animal testing on their products, as they want consumer approval; the Body Shop led the campaign to have the testing of cosmetics on animals banned.

◆ The reduction of packaging on goods and the recycling of packaging materials to protect the environment. Companies want consumer approval so will advertise on the packaging itself the fact that they recycle their packaging. Again the Body Shop was a leader in recycling its packaging, as well as reducing the amount of packaging and labelling of its products.

KEY POINTS

■ Companies can be constrained by:
 – **voluntary codes of practice**
 – **pressure groups**
 – public opinion.

BUSINESS IN PRACTICE

Ribena 'Toothkind' was an innovative development in the soft drinks market. GlaxoSmithKline, the manufacturers of Ribena, spent a long period of time testing the product before its launch to prove that the drink, which contained added calcium to counter the effect of fruit acids on teeth, did help to minimise tooth decay.

After extensive research these facts were proved to the satisfaction of the British Dental Association (BDA), and GlaxoSmithKline earned the right to display the BDA's stamp of approval on Ribena Toothkind cartons. However, the Advertising Standards Authority (ASA) ruled that the Ribena claims were misleading because Ribena Toothkind was only *less harmful* than other sugary drinks, rather than not harmful at all.

The ASA took action after complaints from action groups such as Action and Information on Sugar and the consumer magazine *Which?*

BBC News website (www.news.bbc.co.uk), 17/01/01

 TALK IT OVER

GlaxoSmithKline spent a great deal of time and money testing the product to gain BDA approval. Why did they do this, do you think? How do you think the court case and publicity will affect sales of Ribena and other soft drinks?

PURPOSES OF MARKET RESEARCH

Businesses need to know what the consumer needs and wants to buy.

Some businesses develop and launch a product, and then embark on a heavy promotion and advertising campaign to *convince* consumers that they want the product. This approach is product-orientated.

Some businesses first *find out* what consumers want, and then develop the product to meet their needs. This approach is market-orientated. Many businesses today think that they are most likely to do well if they are market-orientated, so they generally listen to what consumers tell them they want.

To find out what the consumer wants, businesses have to carry out market research – they gather, present, analyse and interpret data about the market's (people's) demands for goods and services.

3	MEDIA

1 How many hours television, on average, do you watch per week?
0-2 hrs 1 ☐ 2-10 hrs 2 ☐ 10-15 hrs 3 ☐ 15+ hrs 4 ☐

2 Which of the following daily newspapers do you read regularly?

Daily Express	01 ☐	Independent	07 ☐
Daily Mail	02 ☐	Star	08 ☐
Daily Mirror	03 ☐	Sun	09 ☐
Daily Telegraph	04 ☐	Times	10 ☐
Financial Times	05 ☐	Today	11 ☐
Guardian	06 ☐	Other	12 ☐

3 Which of the following Sunday newspapers do you read regularly?

Independent on Sunday	01 ☐	Sunday Mirror	07 ☐
Mail on Sunday	02 ☐	Sunday Post	08 ☐
News of the World	03 ☐	Sunday Telegraph	09 ☐
Observer	04 ☐	Sunday Times	10 ☐
Sunday Express	05 ☐	The People	11 ☐
Sunday Mail	06 ☐	Other	12 ☐

4 What kinds of books do you like to read?

Fiction		Non-fiction	
Classical	01 ☐	Biography	09 ☐
Contemporary	02 ☐	Cookery	10 ☐
Crime	03 ☐	Gardening	11 ☐
Fantasy	04 ☐	History	12 ☐
Romance	05 ☐	Popular Science	13 ☐
Science Fiction	06 ☐	Travel	14 ☐
Western	07 ☐	War	15 ☐
Other	08 ☐	Other	16 ☐

BUSINESS IN PRACTICE

Many business organisations ask customers to complete a questionnaire to find out whether they are satisfied with the business's service.

Asda places questionnaires at each checkout (the point-of-sale), where customers can pick them up, complete them and return them. Asda uses the slogan 'We're listening' to assure customers that the business will listen, and act upon, people's comments.

 TALK IT OVER

Why is it important for businesses to know what customers think?

METHODS OF MARKET RESEARCH

There are several ways of collecting market research data. Some large businesses have their own marketing department, whilst others employ outside agencies to do the research for them.

The two main methods of market research are:

◆ **desk research** – gathering together existing data
◆ **field research** – collecting new data directly from the consumer.

KEY POINTS

■ To find out what consumers want or need, a company has to do **market research**.

BUSINESS IN PRACTICE

Boots The Chemists plc uses a wide range of market research methods to find out about customers' buying habits.

To find out about different markets – for example, the digital camera market or the market for cosmetics – Boots uses secondary sources such as MINTEL and Euromonitor.

Primary or field research is used to find out about Boots customers' buying habits. Methods include *observation*, in which customers are watched as they shop; and *omnibus surveys*, which involve short, face-to-face interviews as people enter or leave the store.

Boots also uses independent market research agencies to conduct *focus groups*. These are used to find out what people think of a product or of packaging ideas, perhaps before products are launched.

Perhaps the best source of information Boots has is its Advantage Card *database*. This contains information about 13 million customers, including their age, gender, likes and dislikes. Because the Advantage card uses smart-card technology, it can record what the customer has bought. This information can help Boots to see whether certain market segments buy the same groups of products. For example, do most people who buy Estée Lauder perfume also buy Estée Lauder cosmetics?

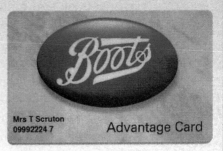

Mrs T Scruton
0999 2224 7   Advantage Card

 ## TALK IT OVER

Compare the advantages and disadvantages of desk research relative to field research.

DESK RESEARCH

Desk research means gathering together *existing* data – data that has already been collected and published for another purpose. This data is called secondary data.

Desk research is a relatively cheap and quick way to gather data that already exists – for example, from the business's own sales figures. Supermarkets use the data collected from their sales tills to identify busy times of day and top-selling products.

Businesses can also use published information. Sources include:

Market research agencies, which collect data, analyse it, and publish the results in journals. This can then be bought by businesses who need information on current consumer markets. MINTEL and Gallup are two such agencies.

The Office of Population Censuses and Surveys carries out a census every ten years on behalf of the government, and this data is available to businesses. It includes such details as age groups in different areas, where people live, and employment statistics.

The government's Office for National Statistics also publishes data – on people's spending (the *Family Expenditure Survey*), and on income and employment (*Social Trends*).

Public libraries have many different types of reference books, and many also have CD-ROM facilities.

Some newspapers and specialist magazines, for example *The Grocer* and *Marketing Weekly*, provide information on market trends.

Internet sites can be useful sources of data, too. For example, the StarUK website lists the top 20 visitor attractions in the UK.

FIELD RESEARCH

Field research gathers new data *direct* from the consumer. The information collected is called primary data. Field research is useful because it

	5 Top Twenty Attractions Charging Admission 1999
1	Alton Towers, Staffordshire
2	Madame Tussaud's, London
3	Tower of London
4	Natural History Museum, London
5	Legoland, Windsor
6	Chessington World of Adventures
7	Science Museum, London
8	Royal Academy, London
9	Canterbury Cathedral
10	Windsor Castle
11	Westminster Abbey
12	Edinburgh Castle
13	Flamingo Land Theme Park, North Yorkshire
14	Drayton Manor Park, Staffordshire
15	Windermere Lake Cruises, Cumbria
16	St. Paul's Cathedral, London
17	London Zoo
18	Chester Zoo
19	Victoria and Albert Museum, London
20	Thorpe Park, Surrey

Note: N/C Not comparable

Source: StarUk, sponsored by the national tourist boards for England, Scotland, Wales, Northern Ireland, the British Tourist Authority and the Department for Culture, Media and Sport

gives the business the exact information it needs, but it is expensive to carry out.

Field research can be carried out in a variety of ways.

◆ **Questionnaires** are often used by businesses. Market researchers are employed to ask questions of the public in face-to-face interviews, either in places such as shopping centres or door-to-door. Alternatively, the questions can be asked over the telephone or the questionnaires can be posted to people's homes.

Face-to-face and telephone interviews require a trained interviewer to ask the questions: this makes them expensive and time-consuming, but it does mean that the interviewer can explain questions if the respondent does not understand them. Postal surveys are cheaper and can cover a wide area, but the **rate of response** is often low.

◆ **Focus groups** can be used. These are small, carefully chosen groups of people who discuss a variety of topics of common interest. It is hoped this will encourage those taking part to be more open about their needs and wants. Focus groups are often used by political parties to find out what policies are popular.

◆ **Consumer panels** are groups of consumers who are asked to test a new product and comment on their findings before the product is put on the open market. This method of research is often used to gauge reaction to new products such as toiletries and food products.

Focus groups and consumer panels each involve only a small number of people, and both are therefore cheap methods of research. However, they may not represent the views of every market segment.

◆ **Test marketing** can be carried out by producing a small run of a new product, and testing it in one small area of the country before opening it up to the full market. Testing in a small area means that customer reactions can be gauged before the business produces the product on a large scale.

KEY POINTS

Market research comprises:

■ **desk research** – using existing data from the business or other sources

■ **field research** – collecting data directly from consumers.

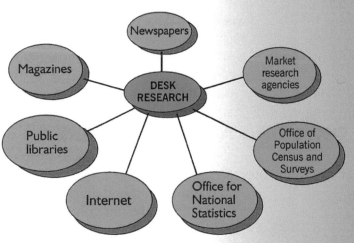

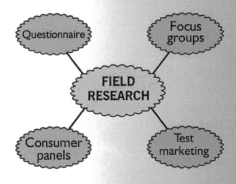

 TALK IT OVER

Why might a business choose desk research instead of field research?

 **Sampling and questionnaires**

METHODS OF SAMPLING

When carrying out market research it is not practical to question *everyone* who might use the product. Businesses would not have the time or the financial or human resources to collect and analyse the results. Businesses therefore try to select a representative sample of the public. Usually a few thousand people will be questioned.

There are two ways to choose a sample:

 random sampling

 quota sampling.

Random sampling does not mean picking just anyone to answer questions. It is a system of selecting people so that everyone has an equal chance of being chosen. The areas in the country that are to be researched are chosen at random, usually by computer. The people to be interviewed are also chosen at random. This can be very time-consuming and it may often give an unbalanced result, as there is no control over the selection of the people being interviewed.

Quota sampling is the method more often used because it is easier to carry out. The market is divided into segments and a certain number of people who fill each segment are deliberately chosen. For example, if 5% of the mobile phone market were female and aged between 17 and 28, then 5% of the survey's sample would be chosen from this group.

DESIGNING A QUESTIONNAIRE

For questionnaires to be useful they must be written with a set objective in mind: for example, to find out whether there is enough demand for a new design of trainers. Questionnaires must have clear, simple, unambiguous questions.

The questions could be closed questions, which means the interviewee is given a limited number of possible answers. The simplest is a question that requires a straight *Yes/No* answer.

1 Which daily newspaper do you usually read?		
Daily	You	Ptnr
Daily Express	01 ☐	28 ☐
Daily Mail	02 ☐	29 ☐
Daily Mirror/Record	03 ☐	30 ☐
Daily Telegraph	04 ☐	31 ☐
Financial Times	05 ☐	32 ☐
Glasgow Herald	06 ☐	33 ☐
Guardian	07 ☐	34 ☐
Independent	08 ☐	35 ☐
Scotsman	09 ☐	36 ☐
Star	10 ☐	37 ☐
Sun	11 ☐	38 ☐
Times	12 ☐	39 ☐
Today	13 ☐	40 ☐
Welsh Times	14 ☐	41 ☐

2 What kind of home do you live in?	
Detached house	1 ☐
Semi-detached house	2 ☐
Terraced House	3 ☐
Flat/Maisonette	4 ☐
Bungalow	5 ☐

3 How many bedrooms does your home have? ☐

4 Is your home	
Owned	1 ☐
Privately rented	2 ☐
Council/Housing Ass.	3 ☐

Extract from a multi-response questionnaire

A closed question can also be a **multi-response question**, which provides the interviewee with a range of possible answers to choose from. For example:

How often do you rent a video?
☐ More than twice a week
☐ Weekly
☐ Less than four times a month

A closed question can ask the interviewee to give an opinion on something on a **scale of preference**, for example to assess a product on a scale of 1 to 5, where

1 = Very poor
3 = Average
5 = Very good

This method is called **attitude scaling**.

The advantage of using closed questions on a questionnaire is that they provide simple, short, positive responses that make the data easy to handle when it is being analysed.

The alternative to a closed question is an **open question**. In this case the interviewee is free to give *any* response. This type of question is difficult to analyse, but could be useful in yielding responses that the researcher has not thought of in advance.

Having written the questionnaire, it should be tested on a small sample of people to check that the questions have been understood and that they are providing the right types of responses. If not, the questionnaire should be modified as necessary, before being used on a full quota of consumers.

KEY POINTS

■ The two main types of **sampling** used for market research are:
– **random**: selecting people and area by random
– **quota**: selecting a set number of people based on age, gender, etc.

■ Good questionnaires:
– should have a set objective
– should be unambiguous
– should be tested before use.

TALK IT OVER

Draw up examples of poor questions. Discuss why they are not ideal, and correct them.

TALK IT OVER

Do you know of anyone who has taken part in market research? Describe what this was and if you think it was appropriate.

TEST YOUR UNDERSTANDING

TOPICS 1–9

1 Why does a business carry out marketing?
2 State the 4Ps of the marketing mix.
3 What is the difference between a market segment and a niche market?
4 Why might a business move into a niche market?
5 Why does a business segment the market?
6 State the two types of market research.
7 What is sampling?
8 Describe three sources of secondary data.
9 Give two reasons why telephone interviews may be better than postal interviews.
10 Explain, using examples, how an open question differs from a closed question.

CASE STUDY

Alton Towers is Britain's number one theme park. It is set in 500 acres of parkland and gardens, which add to the fantasy and magic.

Amusements have been part of Alton Towers since the 1980s. 'The Corkscrew' was the first ride offered to 'thrill-seekers'.

Since the 1980s Alton Towers has tried to balance park developments to meet the needs of both target markets – families and thrill-seekers.

Features of the park include white-knuckle rides such as 'Nemesis' and 'Oblivion', gentle water rides, a themed hotel, a farm, a pub, and live shows.

Many of the family-orientated features were introduced in the early 1990s when a drop in the number of 15–20-year-olds in the population meant that Alton Towers, if it was to keep sales high, needed to focus on other target markets.

The £12 million 'Oblivion' was introduced in 1998 to regain the thrill-seeker target market. This ride had the unique selling proposition (USP) of being the world's first vertical-drop rollercoaster.

The launch of 'Oblivion' was shrouded in secrecy. It was heavily advertised on television to target teenagers, but at the same time Alton Towers used magazines and press releases to target families. Joint promotions, such as vouchers in *The Sun*, were used to encourage families to use the park at quieter, off-peak times. A variety of promotions and advertising had to be used to cater for the very different target markets.

TV Choice: *Marketing a Theme Park* (video), 1998

1 Describe the two main target markets of Alton Towers.

2 Which features named in the passage are aimed (a) at the thrill-seekers, and (b) at families?

3 What does USP stand for, and what does it mean?

4 Who will benefit from promotions such as the vouchers in *The Sun*, which encourage people to use the park at off-peak times?

5 What marketing objectives might Alton Towers have?

EXAM PRACTICE

TipTopTogs is a small but exclusive fashion design business. *Strictly speaking, the fashion business is product-orientated rather than market-orientated*, but TipTopTogs appointed a market research agency to investigate the market for fashion accessories for men.

The market research agency conducted both field and desk research, and some of the results are shown below.

Do you buy designer clothes?

Yes 27%

No 73%

Do you wear co-ordinated outfits?

No 51%

Yes 49%

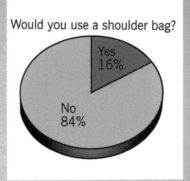

Would you use a shoulder bag?

Yes 16%

No 84%

1 Explain carefully the purpose of market research.   [*3 marks*]

2 Explain why TipTopTogs used a market research agency rather than
conducting the market research themselves.   [*3 marks*]

3 Use examples to explain the difference between *desk research* and *field research*. [*4 marks*]

4 What do the graphs tell us about men's attitudes towards clothing?
Explain your answer.   [*6 marks*]

5 Should TipTopTogs develop fashion accessories for men?
Give reasons for your answer.   [*4 marks*]

1 Read the information above. Explain what is meant by the statement in
italics in the text.   [*4 marks*]

2 Explain the difference between *desk research* and *field research*.   [*3 marks*]

3 The market research agency gathered information using a quota sample.
Explain why this method of sampling was used.   [*5 marks*]

4 Write a brief report advising TipTopTogs on whether or not they
should consider developing fashion accessories for men.   [*8 marks*]

The whole purpose of marketing is to find out what the consumer needs and wants, and to satisfy that demand. The product must have features that make it attractive to the consumer.

MAIN FEATURES

The features that make up an attractive product include such things as:

- Reliability – The product must be fit for the purpose for which it was designed, and do its job well. For example, the VW Golf motor car is well known for its sturdiness.
- Quality – The product must be of a certain standard. For example, Sainsbury's always prides itself on the quality of its goods.
- Value for money – The product must provide good value compared with goods produced by competitors. For example, Tesco, with all the extra facilities it provides for its customers, is currently the leader in the supermarket race to provide the customer with the complete shopping experience.
- Design – The size, colour, weight and shape should be attractive and appropriate to the product. For example, IKEA furniture is modern, colourful and innovative in design.
- Image – The product should create an image that appeals to the customer. For example, the perfume Chanel No. 5 has a glamorous image.
- Status – The product may be bought because the consumers feel it gives them added status. Fashionable sportswear often becomes so because of its association with top sports.

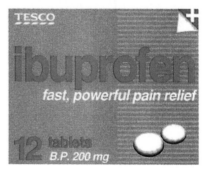

OTHER FEATURES

Other features can be added to a product to make it
more attractive to the consumer, such as:

◆ **Pre-sales service** such as credit facilities. To help
the consumer buy the product, the retailer may
offer **credit**, allowing payment to be spread over a
period of time. This can vary from 0 per cent
finance to no deposit or 3–5 years to pay. This is
used for expensive items such as cars and furniture.

◆ **After-sales service**. Machinery and equipment
can be sold with the facility to have the products
serviced after they have been purchased. For
example, when buying a new car the
manufacturer will recommend that the car is
serviced after a set period of time, or after so
many miles of use. The first service is often free
as an added incentive.

◆ **Manuals**. For equipment such as computers,
video recorders or dishwashers, which need to be
properly operated, instruction books on assembly
and use are provided.

◆ **Guarantees**. Some products have guarantees
against wearing out over a certain period after
the purchase. If it does, the company may replace
the entire product or simply repair it. Guarantees
are also used as a sign of quality – on some foods,
for example.

KEY POINTS

■ The most important part
of the marketing mix is
the product.

■ Features which make an
attractive product
include:
– reliability
– quality
– value for money
– design
– image
– status.

■ Products can have extra
features to make them
more appealing such as:
– pre-sales service
– after-sales service
– manuals
– guarantees.

MONEY BACK GUARANTEE
IF YOU OR YOUR FAMILY ARE IN ANY WAY DISAPPOINTED WITH THIS
PRODUCT, PLEASE RETURN THE BEST BEFORE PANEL, STATING YOUR
REASONS AND WHERE AND WHEN BOUGHT, TO THE ADDRESS BELOW.
THIS DOES NOT AFFECT YOUR STATUTORY RIGHTS.
BIRDS EYE WALL'S LIMITED, WALTON-ON-THAMES,
SURREY, ENGLAND KT12 1NT.
IN EIRE CONTACT: BIRDS EYE FOODS (IRELAND) LTD,
WHITEHALL ROAD, RATHFARNHAM, DUBLIN 14.

℮ NET WEIGHT 375g 13.2oz

CUSTOMER SERVICE

An area to which businesses pay a lot of attention is
customer service. This includes anything in
addition to the product that meets the customer's
needs. Some examples are baby-changing facilities in
Marks & Spencer's, home delivery from Iceland
stores, and free newspapers in McDonald's.

 TALK IT OVER

Why do businesses spend
so much money on staff
training and customer
service facilities?

Any new product will have an expected life cycle. This is the length of time the manufacturer expects the product to sell. This life cycle is made up of a series of stages.

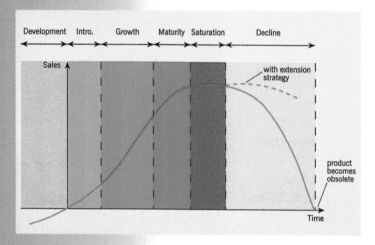

STAGES OF A PRODUCT LIFE CYCLE

Stage 1 – Development

The business invests a lot of money into researching the market for the new product, developing the product, and market-testing the product. At this stage of the life cycle the product is making no money for the company: on the contrary, it is costing money for the development.

Stage 2 – Introduction

The product is launched on the market. A promotion campaign and a large amount of advertising will take place at this stage. The product is still making a loss for the business, as sales are low.

Stage 3 – Growth

The product becomes known in the market: sales should start to increase. Advertising is continued, but less frequently than at the launch. The product should begin to make a profit.

Stage 4 – Maturity

The product is now well established in the market. Promotion will be used to remind the consumer

 TALK IT OVER

Think of a range of different products, consider how long they have been around and if relevant, how these products have changed.

Sometimes a company may restyle a product to extend its life cycle a little bit longer

about the product. This is when the product reaches its highest sales and profit levels. At this stage the business may use an **extension strategy** (see below) to prolong maturity.

Stage 5 – Saturation

The market for the product becomes **saturated**. The only way to increase sales at this stage is to take them from competitors. Promotion strategies are used to do this. At this stage the business may also use an extension strategy to delay the product's decline.

Stage 6 – Decline

The product begins to lose its competitive edge. More rival products are introduced into the market. The product has become out of date. Sales begin to fall. Profits also begin to fall. When the product is no longer wanted, it is **obsolete**.

EXTENSION STRATEGIES

A successful extension strategy will delay a product's decline. Strategies include:

◆ **product development** – making changes to the product to make it more appealing

◆ **market development** – finding new markets for existing products, for example Lucozade is now aimed at athletes as well as people who are ill

◆ **widening the product range** – producing more varieties of the same product, for instance cola-flavoured Smarties, or strawberry Milky Ways.

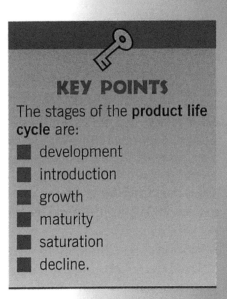

KEY POINTS

The stages of the **product life cycle** are:

■ development

■ introduction

■ growth

■ maturity

■ saturation

■ decline.

BUSINESS IN PRACTICE

Bensons crisps are one of the products manufactured by Snackhouse plc. The company also produces XL crisps, Beano, Rugrats and Thomas the Tank Engine snacks.

In 2000 Snackhouse launched no fewer than four new products:

- The Captain Organic range (healthy snacks for kids) was launched in May.
- Director's Cut (premium-quality snacks for adults) were also launched in May.
- In June The Simpsons snack products

were introduced onto the market.

- Launched to coincide with the sci-fi animation **Titan AE**, the Titan AE snack was launched in July.

Website: www.snackhouse.co.uk

 TALK IT OVER

Bringing out new products can be expensive and risky. Why do businesses bring out new products so frequently?

A brand name is associated with large, long-established companies such as Kellogg's or BMW. These companies have well-known products which are instantly distinguishable from their competitors – that is, they achieve product differentiation. They also have attributes associated with their brand names. BMW, for example, is associated with quality and status.

A brand name can apply to a product, such as Nescafé, or to a business, such as Nestlé.

CREATING A BRAND NAME

To create a brand name, the business must start with a very good product and distinguish this from its rivals. This might be achieved by making the design of the packaging bold, attractive and instantly recognisable; or through advertising, so that the consumer relates the name to good and consistent high quality. Logos are also used – for example, all car companies have a symbol that they put on their cars.

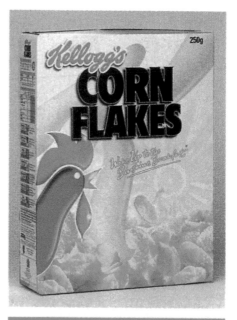

A brand name is associated with long-established companies

BRAND LOYALTY

By creating this brand image the manufacturer hopes to create brand loyalty also, encouraging the consumer to continue to buy its own products in preference to those of its rivals.

If the manufacturer is able to develop a strong brand name, it may be able to sell its products at a premium price – a price higher than those of its competitors. The consumer is prepared to pay the higher price because he or she feels that the branded product is of a higher quality; and branded products are advertised more widely, so the consumer is more aware of their existence.

If the manufacturer has a strong brand image, it may be able to transfer the customer's loyalty to other goods it makes. For example, Mars and Bounty chocolate bars have been very successfully developed into ice cream bars.

 TALK IT OVER

Procter & Gamble produces several different brands of soap powder, including Bold 2 in 1, Dreft, Ariel and Tide. Why do you think it is more profitable to do this than to produce only one brand?

OWN-BRAND GOODS

Own-brand labels are goods that carry the name of the retailer that sells them. For example, Asda, Sainsbury and Tesco all sell their own-brand label goods. They are in direct competition with the named-brand goods such as Kellogg's, which they also sell on their shelves.

Many supermarkets already sold their own-brand goods for some items, for example cornflakes and baked beans. The most important attraction of these goods was their lower price. Businesses such as Kwik Save have taken this idea one stage further, advertising 'no frills' goods at even lower prices.

Often own-brand goods were not as good as the brand-name goods. Then supermarkets became more competitive with each other, and had to improve the quality of their own-brand goods. Sometimes they even had the manufacturers of branded goods making the same goods especially for them!

KEY POINTS

- **Brand names** identify a product.
- Retailers sell **own-brand goods**, which are often cheaper than competitors' brands.
- A **brand name** is a way of achieving **product differentiation**.

BUSINESS IN PRACTICE

Many people were surprised when Sainsbury's decided to launch its own-brand cola. Everyone felt that Pepsi and Coke (Coca Cola) had cornered the market, and no other brand could touch them.

But they were wrong. Sainsbury's spent time and money developing a good (and cheaper) own-brand cola, and their sales rocketed. Since then business people have realised that own-brand goods can compete with, and beat, branded goods. The fact that Sainsbury's has a reputation for quality goods also helped it win over consumers.

 TALK IT OVER

Are brand-name goods marketed differently from unbranded or own-brand goods?

IMPORTANCE OF PACKAGING

Packaging is important in delivering goods to the consumer in a safe, hygienic condition. Cakes, for example, often have several layers of packaging to protect them from being crushed and to make sure that they reach the consumer in a good condition. Further packaging may be needed to help the retailers store the products easily and safely on the shelves.

The packaging may be used by the manufacturer to promote the goods, as the colour, design or lettering may make the product more attractive and noticeable to the consumer on the shelf.

The packaging can also be used to pass on details of contents, ingredients, weight, care instructions, and the like. Some of these are now a statutory requirement.

Packaging can provide details of ingredients

PROBLEMS OF PACKAGING

Packaging can create problems for the manufacturer, as it adds to the cost of producing the goods. Excessive packaging has also been a source of complaint from consumers in recent years, as they have become more sensitive to environmental issues. The packaging creates problems with its use of natural resources and with its disposal afterwards. Many companies have now undertaken to **recycle** as much of their packaging as possible.

KEY POINTS

- Good packaging is an important part of the product.

 TALK IT OVER

What problems for these businesses may have been caused by changing to recycled packaging? Why will businesses have thought it worthwhile to deal with these problems?

BUSINESS IN PRACTICE

In 1989 McDonald's and the USA's Environmental Defence Fund formed an agreement to work together.

'Our goal is to ensure that as much of the material remaining in the restaurants after use ends up in a sensible recovery or recycling stream,' said Else Kreuck, McDonald's Environmental Manager in Europe.

Ten years on McDonald's has had huge success, making improvements in packaging to cause less damage to the environment.

In stores they have used more recycled materials, switching from foam cartons to paper wraps for burgers and cutting the size of straws and napkins to reduce materials used.

McDonald's has also made improvements behind the counter, and influenced businesses in the supply chain to become more environmentally friendly. They even use chairs and tables made from recycled materials!

 TALK IT OVER

A reduction in packaging materials will lead to savings for McDonald's, but how else could their improvements boost sales?

IS THE PRICE RIGHT?

Businesses use marketing to find out consumers' needs and wants, so that they can react and provide for those needs and wants.

The business is in control of the products it makes and sells. It does not have as much control over the price it charges for its products. There are three important factors that affect the price a business can charge. These are:

- the actual cost of making the goods
- the price charged for similar goods in the marketplace
- conditions in the market at which the product is aimed.

An organisation will not stay in business very long if it makes a loss on every item it sells. Nor will it stay in business very long if it charges four times as much as its competitors for similar products.

COST-PLUS PRICING

Cost-plus pricing means taking into account the costs of making the product. It is based on the direct costs of producing the goods and a percentage of the indirect costs such as overheads – rent, heating, and so on. A percentage mark-up is then added on to calculate the selling price. The amount to be added may be worked out by taking into account the market demand for the goods and the price being charged by the business's competitors.

It is often difficult, however, to work out exactly what one item costs to make. Most large organisations employ management accountants to help with pricing, but here is a simplified version of how it might work:

A manufacturer makes a pair of jeans:

	£
Material	15
Labour	10
Share of overheads	15
Unit cost	40

Buy 1 bottle of shampoo
Get 1 bottle of conditioner
half price!

Buy 6 videos and get
15%
discount

100
EXTRA
POINTS
**If you buy
2 JARS**

3 for the price of 2!

Today only!
save up to 50%
on selected
TVs and videos

The manufacturer marks up all its retail prices by 50%, which gives it a retail selling price of £60.

The profit margin is the difference between the selling price and the unit cost. In this case the profit margin is £20.

COMPETITION-BASED PRICING

In competition-based pricing the business sets its selling price at a level similar to that of its competitors, even if this means a smaller profit margin.

When a new product is brought onto the market, the business may decide to sell its product at a lower price than that of its competitors to begin with, to gain a larger share of the market. This is called penetration pricing.

Destroyer pricing involves selling goods at a very low price to try to destroy competition. In recent years many of the national newspapers have used this type of pricing to reduce competition. The Times sold its newspaper at 10p a copy for a period of time, when competitors were charging 40–50p per copy, to try to attract customers to buy its product.

MARKET-ORIENTATED PRICING

When a market chooses its price to take advantage of market conditions, it is said to be using market-orientated pricing.

The opposite of penetration pricing is creaming or skimming. This is when the business sets its prices high to begin with, and then lowers the price later on. This is often used with new, high-technology products. Computers, calculators, video cameras and digital cameras were all very expensive to buy when they first came on the market. They were made for a niche market – people who were very often enthusiasts, and willing to pay a high price. Then, in order to attract a wider audience and get into the mass market, manufacturers reduced their prices.

KEY POINTS

- The factors that influence the **price** of a product are:
  - the manufacturing cost
  - the price of similar products
  - the effect of price on the market.
- The manufacturing cost is calculated by:
  - **direct costs** – costs related to the product, such as raw materials
  - **indirect costs** – costs related to overheads.
- **Competition-based pricing** – setting prices similar to those of competitors.
- **Penetration pricing** – setting prices lower to increase market share.
- **Creaming** or **skimming** – setting prices higher to appeal to a niche market.
- **Destroyer pricing** – setting prices very low to drive competitors out of business.
- **Cost-plus pricing** – setting prices based entirely on the manufacturing cost.
- **Profit margin** – the difference between the cost of producing one unit and the selling price.
- **Mark-up** – the amount by which the cost of producing one unit is increased, usually expressed as a percentage: for example, a 10% mark-up on a product that costs £100 gives a selling price of £110.

VALUE ADDED TAX

Value Added Tax (VAT) must be added to most goods and services. There are exceptions, such as basic foods, children's clothes and footwear, books and newspapers. VAT is a tax levied by the government, at a rate of 17.5% in the UK for most products.

CUSTOMS AND EXCISE DUTIES

The government puts customs and excise duties on a range of goods such as alcohol, tobacco and petrol, and Stamp Duty on the sale of houses. These all have to be added to the price of the goods – the business has no choice in this.

ECONOMIC POLICY

The general economy of the country can also affect prices, depending on the government's economic policies and other factors such as inflation (see Unit 1, Topic 17, for more details).

EXCHANGE RATE

The exchange rate for the pound can also affect the price of goods and services. The exchange rate is the value of the pound when buying foreign currencies.

If the pound is strong (worth more against foreign currencies), businesses have more money to spend when buying goods from abroad. However, it is more difficult to sell abroad, because the strong pound makes UK goods more expensive to buy in foreign countries.

The changes in the value of the pound against foreign currencies can have a great influence on prices, but businesses have no control over exchange rates: they just have to accept them and adapt their prices to match the changes in exchange rates.

CONSUMERS' EXPECTATIONS

There are many products that have approximately the same costs of production yet are sold at a wide range of prices.

'Look at all the tax and duty I've saved!'

Sometimes the products have extra features, but generally these 'extras' do not explain the price difference. In fact, this difference is usually because the seller charges the price that the consumer expects to pay.

For example, the price charged for a 50 ml bottle of perfume can range from a few pounds to around £50, or even more. Although the costs of production will be approximately the same in each case, the producer charges what the consumer expects to pay – and some people would not admit to paying less than £30 for a bottle of perfume!

DEMAND AND SUPPLY

When demand for a good increases or the good is in short supply, the price tends to rise. Similarly, when demand falls or there is a surplus of a good, the price tends to fall.

KEY POINTS

■ Other outside factors can affect costs, such as:
 – taxes
 – inflation
 – exchange rates
 – demand and supply.

TALK IT OVER

Can you think of other examples of products for which the price charged is that which the consumer expects to pay?

BUSINESS IN PRACTICE

September 2000 saw the population grind to a halt as fuel for cars and lorries became unavailable. Lorry drivers felt that the price of fuel was too high and, as a protest, blockaded refineries to restrict supply.

Petrol stations either put up their prices or sold out very quickly. Queues of motorists could be seen at every petrol station that still had fuel. The NHS was put on red alert and fire engines were refuelled under a police guard.

The increased price of fuel was partly because OPEC countries were restricting supply, but also because of the tax the government had levied on fuel.

Lorry drivers asked the government to reduce the tax on fuel in the next budget.

Website: www.telegraph.co.uk

(from *Electronic Telegraph*)

TALK IT OVER

How did OPEC cause the price of oil to rise? If fuel is more expensive, how might this affect businesses?

DEMAND

Before producing a product, a business needs to know how much of it people would buy. This information can be collected using market research. The amount of a given product that people would buy is called the demand.

THE DEMAND CURVE

Usually the demand for a product will be higher if the price is lower. The table shows the quantity of CDs students in a school would buy (per month) at various prices.

From this information a demand curve can be plotted. This shows the same information in a different way.

TALK IT OVER

Why might 80 people be prepared to pay £20?

Price	Quantity
£5	200
£10	160
£15	120
£20	80

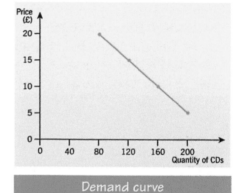

Demand curve

SUPPLY

Producers of a product will produce quantities of a product according to how much people are willing to pay. The amount produced is called the supply.

If customers are willing to pay £15 for a CD, producers are more encouraged to supply CDs than if customers were only willing to pay £5. Usually as price goes up, supply goes up.

THE SUPPLY CURVE

The table shows the quantity of CDs a producer is willing to supply (per month) for a number of different prices.

From this information a supply curve can be plotted, showing the same information in a different way.

Price	Quantity
£5	80
£10	100
£15	120
£20	140

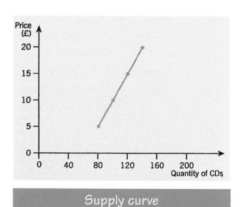

Supply curve

MARKET PRICE

The market price for a product is often the price that is charged. This is the price at which demand and supply are equal – in this case, £15.

 TALK IT OVER

How do demand and supply work in an auction?

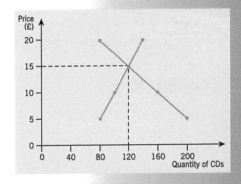

Market price

FACTORS THAT AFFECT DEMAND AND SUPPLY

Demand can be affected by a number of factors, such as advertising, incomes, and prices of other goods. If demand goes up because of any of these factors, market price will rise.

Supply can be affected by a number of factors, such as the cost of labour or the cost of raw materials. If supply goes down for any reason, the market price will rise.

 TALK IT OVER

Think of a range of products. Discuss what factors might affect the demand for and supply of these products.

PRICE IN REAL LIFE

In a very competitive market businesses may find that they cannot choose the price that they would prefer: they may have no choice but to accept the market price.

Often prices for particular products vary very little from one business to another. For example, petrol prices vary only by a few pence per litre. This is because every business must accept the market price.

However, businesses may use penetration pricing or destroyer pricing and go below the market price for a short while. Similarly, they may charge a premium price above the market price if they feel they have established brand loyalty.

KEY POINTS

■ **Demand** – the quantity of a product that will be bought at a given price.

■ **Supply** – the quantity of a product that will be produced at a given price.

■ **Market price** – the price at which the quantity of a product demanded is equal to the quantity that suppliers are willing to produce.

TEST YOUR UNDERSTANDING

TOPICS 10–16

1 What is a **brand name**?
2 Explain why brand loyalty may be good for business.
3 In the introduction and decline stages of the product life cycle, sales are low. Explain how the two stages are different.
4 Describe the saturation stage of the product life cycle.
5 What is an **extension strategy**? Give two examples.
6 What is the purpose of packaging?
7 How can packaging affect the sales of a product?
8 State two requirements for the packaging of pickled onions.
9 What is meant by **cost-plus pricing**?
10 If a product sells for £10 and has a 25% mark-up, what is the cost price?

CASE STUDY

Cadbury Schweppes is a global company which manufactures and distributes branded products in over 200 countries. Following the merger of Cadbury (chocolate) and Trebor Bassett (sweets) Cadbury Trebor Bassett is Cadbury Schweppes' UK confectionery operation.

The Cadbury business was founded in 1842 by John Cadbury. He began manufacturing cocoa and drinking chocolate because he believed that if people had an alternative to drinking alcohol there would be less misery and hardship among the poor.

Since 1842 Cadbury has gone from strength to strength. The confectionery market has grown because chocolate has become cheaper and because of lifestyle changes which mean that people 'snack' on chocolate. But competition is intense.

Cadbury has continually invested money into research and development for new and innovative products. Many products do not make it to the introduction stage of the product life cycle and are never launched; others have been around for years and still sell well. Marble and Astros are examples of recent Cadbury launches, but perhaps the most successful launch recently has been Fuse (see www.cadbury.co.uk/today/fuse). Cadbury's Dairy Milk was launched in 1905 and is still the top-selling brand in the UK. Newer products such as Miniature Heroes are gaining popularity as people's awareness and brand loyalty grow.

Cadbury also tries to get the most out of its existing brands by launching new varieties, for example Wispa Gold and the limited-edition Lemonade Crunchie. The Cadbury's Dairy Milk megabrand is a development of the original bar.

To gain a competitive advantage Cadbury must ensure that its product has a unique selling proposition (USP) – something that makes the product different from all other chocolate bars on the shelf.

1 Explain the terms: (a) **product development**; (b) **unique selling proposition** (USP).

2 Why does Cadbury have so many products in its portfolio?

3 Sketch the product life cycles of three Cadbury products. How do they differ?

4 Why do some products not survive past the development stage?

5 Suggest three ways in which Cadbury could develop an existing product.

EXAM PRACTICE

Street Fun Ltd is a small company manufacturing equipment for street games. The life cycle of roller blades, one of their current products, is shown here.

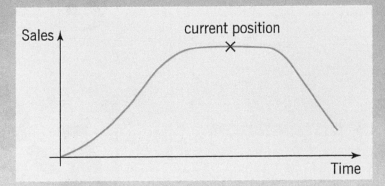

1 Explain the difference between **penetration pricing** and **skimming**. [4 marks]

2 Describe two situations when a firm might use: (a) penetration pricing; (b) skimming. [4 marks]

3 What could happen to make demand for roller blades fall **other** than a change in price. [6 marks]

4 Describe some extension strategies that could be used when the roller blades are in the maturity/saturation stage of their life cycle. [6 marks]

1 Explain which pricing strategy Street Fun Ltd would have used during the launch and growth of the roller blades. [4 marks]

2 Explain which pricing strategy the marketing director should be using now. [4 marks]

3 Discuss the factors **other** than a change in price that could affect the demand for roller blades. Suggest how Street Fun Ltd could react to these changes in demand. [12 marks]

Getting the product to the right place involves two decisions: choosing the right *place* to sell the product and deciding the best way to get the product to the market (also called **distribution** or **placement**). This part of the marketing mix is called **place**.

IMPORTANCE OF DISTRIBUTION

Unless a business gets the product to the place where the customer will see it and buy it, all the other work done – designing the product, choosing the right price, and promoting the product – is useless.

Effective **distribution** needs business decisions on:

which channels of distribution to use – wholesaler, retailer, customer

which method of distribution to use – road, rail, air, sea.

CHANNELS OF DISTRIBUTION

The types of organisation a manufacturer uses to get its products to the customer are called the **channel of distribution**. A traditional channel of distribution uses a wholesaler and a retailer. Other channels of distribution may miss out the retailer, the wholesaler, or both.

A channel of distribution that involves *only* the manufacturer and the customer is called **direct selling**.

It is important that the manufacturer finds the most effective channel to distribute its goods to the consumer. In general, the *shorter* the link between manufacturer and customer, the *cheaper* it is to distribute the product, and therefore the *lower* the price of the product can be. More links in the channel of distribution mean more expensive goods, because there are more people involved who will want part of the profit for handling these goods.

A long distance from the manufacturer to the next link in the channel of distribution increases the cost of transporting the goods. There is also more chance of damage to the goods, or theft. Perishable goods

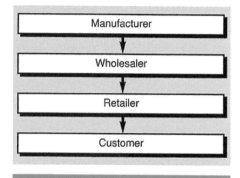

Channel of distribution

have to be moved very quickly if they are to reach the consumer in good condition.

Many manufacturers, including Kellogg's, use wholesalers or regional distribution centres (see Unit 2, Topic 19) to distribute their goods.

FUNCTIONS OF THE WHOLESALER

It is expensive for manufacturers to sell small quantities of goods direct to retailers, so traditionally they use a wholesaler. Wholesalers buy goods in large quantities from the manufacturer, often receiving discounts for the size of their orders. The goods are sold on to retailers in smaller quantities. This is called breaking bulk.

Wholesalers increase costs of distribution as they are an additional link. Some wholesalers offer transport and credit facilities to retailers.

FUNCTIONS OF THE RETAILER

The retailer offers consumers convenience, by bringing goods to a nearby location, and by allowing purchase of small quantities. Retailers also offer credit and after-sales service.

KEY POINTS

■ Decisions about **place** include:
– where goods are sold
– how goods are distributed.
These decisions are sometimes called the **placement** or **distribution** of the product.

■ **Channel of distribution** – the route that goods follow from manufacturer to consumer.

■ The main functions of the **wholesaler** are:
– to break bulk
– to offer credit and delivery services.

■ The main function of the **retailer** is:
– to provide convenience.

BUSINESS IN PRACTICE

How does a bag of crisps find its way to the customer?

Walkers' products are manufactured at six different factories located throughout the UK. From these factories Walkers delivers more than 70 million cases of crisps and snacks to more than 9000 individual outlets. These outlets range from corner shops and petrol stations to public houses and hypermarkets, as far north as Fraserburgh in Scotland and as far south as Penzance in Cornwall.

Walkers makes use of its own five distribution centres located throughout the UK: in Bristol, Enfield, Leicester, Lincoln and Warrington. A

fleet of 200 vehicles transports the crisps and snacks by road from the factories to the distribution centres, and then to the retailers.

It is a network that works 24 hours a day, and a fleet that covers 18 million miles per year to bring us our crisps and snacks.

Walkers Snack Foods Information Booklet

 TALK IT OVER

What advantages and disadvantages are there to Walkers of using its own fleet of lorries and distribution centres?

TYPES OF RETAILER

Goods can be sold to the consumer through a wide variety of different outlets.

A **vending machine** sells goods direct to the consumer. The goods are purchased by putting the correct money into the machine and choosing an item from the goods on display: the goods are then ejected from the machine. Vending machines are found in bus stations and in shopping centres, and are useful when shops are closed.

A **mobile shop** is often used in country areas where there are not many shops. Mobile shops can sell fruit and vegetables, fresh fish, fresh meat, and so on. They travel round the streets to sell their goods.

A **market** is a series of stalls, usually on open ground and held once or twice a week. Markets can sell a range of goods, from food to clothes to furniture.

An **independent store** is a small shop, usually owned and run by one person.

A **chain store** is a group of stores selling the same range of goods in a number of different towns and cities. Examples are Marks & Spencer and Woolworth.

A **department store** is a large store, usually in the town centre. It sells a wide range of goods, and often leases floor space to other companies to sell *within* its stores. Some Debenham's department stores, for example, have a Kookai outlet in them – this is not part of the Debenham's company: it is just using the store.

A **supermarket** is a large store, usually selling mainly food items and some household goods.

A **hypermarket** sells food as well as other products. Hypermarkets are all on one floor, and increasingly are located in out-of-town centres, with car parking facilities alongside. Other customer facilities may include a photograph booth, a baby room, a cafeteria, and even a toddlers' play area. Tesco and Asda are examples.

KEY POINTS

Consumers can be sold goods through:

- vending machines
- mobile shops
- markets
- independent shops
- chain stores
- department stores
- supermarkets
- hypermarkets
- discount warehouses
- shopping malls.

◆ A **discount warehouse** is a large retail store in which the prices are usually lower than those in other stores selling similar goods. Discount warehouses are often located on the outskirts of the town, and sell such things as DIY goods, electrical goods or car accessories. B&Q, Curry's and PC World are examples.

◆ A **shopping mall** is a collection of different shops and owners, gathered under one roof. They have their own free car parking facilities, and offer a wide range of goods and services to the public, such as restaurants and bars, crèche facilities, and direct transport links with all the local areas. Examples of large shopping malls are the MetroCentre in Newcastle, the Trafford Centre in Manchester, Meadowhall in Sheffield and Lakeside in Essex.

 TALK IT OVER

What are the differences between the different types of retail outlets you have visited?

Meadowhall, Sheffield

There are several different methods of distributing goods other than the 'traditional' route using wholesalers and retailers.

DIRECT SELLING

Many small manufacturers sell direct to the consumer. Examples are craftspeople such as painters, potters and sculptors.

MAIL ORDER

Mail order is another method of direct selling. The manufacturer produces a catalogue of goods, and the consumer buys direct from the manufacturer. Goods are delivered by courier or delivery service. Grattans, Kays and the Next Directory are all examples of companies that sell direct to their customers via a mail-order catalogue. The Internet is also a rapidly developing high-tech electronic mail-order e-commerce facility (see 'Business in practice', opposite).

NETWORK MARKETING

Some manufacturers use a network of people to distribute their goods to family and friends by holding parties or meetings in their houses. It is hoped that some of the people attending the party will then volunteer to hold another party: this is how the network continues to develop. Tupperware and Avon cosmetics have been sold for many years using this method.

 TALK IT OVER

What are the advantages of mail order?

WAREHOUSE CLUBS

The idea of warehouse clubs has been brought over from the USA. The warehouses sell goods in bulk. Members of the public pay a fee to shop in these outlets – you cannot buy goods in the warehouses unless you are a member. An example of a warehouse club is Costco.

Costco is an example of a warehouse club

CASH-AND-CARRY WAREHOUSES

Cash-and-carry warehouses were originally wholesalers selling goods on to small retailers. They broke bulk from large manufacturers and the small retailers bought from them, paid cash, and took the goods away to sell to consumers. No delivery service was offered by the wholesalers.

This idea has now been expanded to include the general public as direct customers. Large warehouse stores have been built in out-of-town shopping centres and sell to small tradespeople as well as the general public.

REGIONAL DISTRIBUTION CENTRES

Regional distribution centres are a form of warehouse. They were originally used by supermarket chains, as a central point where goods could be stored and from which they could be delivered to the supermarkets in that particular region. Manufacturers all delivered their goods to the distribution centre by road, and then the supermarket chains used their own fleets of lorries to deliver the goods to their outlets in that particular region.

This idea has grown in recent years, with independent companies setting up distribution centres to deliver a manufacturer's goods for it in the different regions of the country.

KEY POINTS

■ **Channels of distribution** include:
– direct selling
– mail order
– network marketing
– warehouse clubs
– cash-and-carries
– regional distribution centres.

■ **E-commerce** – buying and selling over the Internet.

BUSINESS IN PRACTICE

EasyJet.com is the world's first ticketless airline. If you want to buy an airline ticket from EasyJet you do not visit your local travel agent, nor make a phone call – you log onto the Internet! This is an example of e-commerce.

Once on the Net customers must first e-mail EasyJet with their details, and can then purchase airline tickets by credit card. Computer software programs check flight availability and issue the customer with a reference number. A receipt is e-mailed to the customer's home computer, where it can be printed out.

When booking in at the airport the customer is given a recyclable ticket in return for the reference number. This ticket is returned to staff on boarding the plane.

The whole transaction takes place without tickets and without a retail outlet.

EasyJet is now expanding its fleet of aircraft and diversifying into EasyRentacar, EasyEverything and EasyMoney. All of these services make full use of direct selling over the Internet.

 **TALK IT OVER**

Why has EasyJet been so successful?

A range of methods are used to transport goods. Each method has its advantages and disadvantages.

Several factors must be considered when deciding which method of transport to use:

The nature of the goods – are they heavy, bulky, perishable?

Time – are the goods needed urgently?

Cost – will it still be possible to make a profit after paying for the transport?

Distance – how far do the goods have to travel?

Available transport – are the goods going overseas?

TALK IT OVER

Why might some businesses have special transport departments?

ROAD

Using road transport means that the company can give door-to-door delivery. This can be contracted out to transport companies, and can be the cheapest and quickest form of delivery over short distances. However, it is subject to traffic jams; lorries can be held up abroad; and drivers can drive for only a set number of hours each day.

RAIL

Rail can be quick and efficient for long distances. It is suitable for large, heavy loads and avoids road congestion, but unless the business has a rail link – as does Alcan in Northumberland, for

example – it cannot deliver to the door. This means that goods have to be loaded and unloaded several times, as road transport will also have to be used to take the goods the last few miles to the customer.

AIR

Distribution by air is fast but probably the most expensive form of transport. It is limited as to the size of cargo it can carry. Air transport is ideally suited to perishable goods such as fresh fruit and flowers, but is not suitable for bulky products.

As with rail transport, road transport may have to be used for the last few miles.

SEA

Sea distribution is cheap for carrying goods very long distances. It is used for transporting heavy, bulky loads that cannot be accommodated by air.

Sea distribution is a slow form of transport. Loads may have to be transferred to lorries for the last few miles, but this is easily done if the goods are in **containers**. Containers are huge rectangular constructions which can be moved between different methods of transport.

KEY POINTS
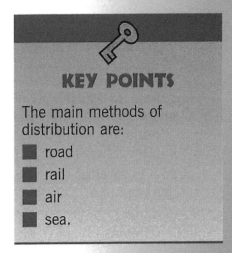

The main methods of distribution are:
- road
- rail
- air
- sea.

TALK IT OVER
How would you transport stereos from Japan to London?

BUSINESS IN PRACTICE

The firm Rhys Davies offers a specialist service in distributing dangerous goods.
Website: www.rhysdavies.co.uk

TALK IT OVER
Why might Zeon Chemicals and Borden Chemicals choose to transport goods by road?

ZEON CHEMICALS

BORDEN CHEMICAL, INC.

Promotion is the fourth part of the marketing mix. It is all about informing the consumer about the product – what it is, what it is for – and then persuading the consumer to buy it.

There are a number of techniques that can be used to promote products:

- sponsorship
- public relations
- packaging
- advertising
- sales promotion.

SPONSORSHIPS

Businesses offer sponsorship to draw people's attention to their name or product. Examples are Vodafone sponsoring Manchester United, or Cadbury's sponsoring *Coronation Street* on television. Sponsorship can also be used at a local level for events such as sports meetings or concerts.

Sponsorship draws attention to companies' names

PUBLIC RELATIONS

Many organisations use public relations as a way of promoting an image of the business as a whole, rather than just one product.

Public relations is a long-term activity: it takes a long time to build up positive images of a whole company. This can be achieved through press releases in newspapers and magazines, or by being involved with local or even national communities, for example by providing equipment for schools.

PACKAGING

Goods need packaging to protect them from damage and to keep the contents in a saleable condition. Packaging is also needed to display weight or volume, ingredients, and cooking instructions for food.

As well as protecting goods, packaging can give instant company recognition

However, packaging can do much more than just protect the goods. It is part of the company's image, and can give instant recognition to the company. It can create an image of basic good-value goods, as with Asda's 'Smart Price' range of goods, or sheer luxury, as with Chanel perfumes. Packaging can be what makes a customer pick these goods off the shelf rather than a competitor's product, because they look so attractive or so different.

KEY POINTS

■ Products can be **promoted** through:
- sponsorship
- public relations
- packaging
- advertising
- sales promotion.

■ Packaging promotion can present an **image** and make goods look more attractive.

BUSINESS IN PRACTICE

WINNERS 2001
ntl: BASKETBALL National Cup

The multinational company ntl provides digital television, Internet access and telephone calls through its communication network. It believes that people should be able to communicate wherever they are and whenever they want, and aims to make it simple for them to do so.

As a company, ntl relies heavily on its sponsorship of television programmes, charities and sports events to raise potential customers' awareness.

Thanks to a recent amendment in communications regulations, ntl is allowed to display its telephone number and web address in television credits. You may have noticed this if you have ever watched *Who Wants To Be A Millionaire?*

It has also teamed up with Yahoo! (an Internet search engine) to sponsor a charity event in London. Many celebrities auctioned their Christmas stockings in aid of the Macmillan Cancer Relief charity.

As well as sponsoring football teams such as Aston Villa, Newcastle United, Celtic and Rangers, ntl have made a commitment to basketball by sponsoring the National Basketball Cup.

Sponsorship for the 2001 Lions' rugby tour of Australia has also been provided by ntl, its logo appearing on team shirts, training kit, official leisure wear and replica merchandise.

Website: www.ntl.co.uk

 TALK IT OVER

It will cost ntl £1 million to sponsor the Lions' rugby tour of Australia. What will ntl gain from this investment?

Advertising is the most widely known form of promotion. It is used to inform and persuade customers to buy a business's product.

Businesses can use a variety of different media to get their advertising message across. Cinema, newspapers, magazines, radio, television, billboards or hoardings, and even public transport, are used for advertising.

Public transport is a popular advertising medium

ADVERTISING MEDIA

The choice of medium is often dictated by the amount of money the business has to spend on advertising. Small businesses are likely to use methods such as:

- word of mouth
- local newspapers
- leaflets
- ◆ *Yellow Pages*
- ◆ public transport
- ◆ catalogues.

These methods are cheap but usually reach only customers in a localised area.

Leaflets are especially useful if a business wants to select whom it reaches, but they may be viewed as junk mail and discarded.

Large businesses, on the other hand, are more likely to use methods such as:

- radio
- television
- the national press
- ◆ specialist trade magazines
- ◆ trade fairs
- ◆ billboards.

The cost of advertising on television is very high. Also, the cost varies immensely depending on the time of day when the advertisement is to be shown. The peak time, between 6.00 pm and 10.00 pm, is the most expensive.

INFORMATIVE AND PERSUASIVE ADVERTISING

The purpose of informative advertising is to give information. Informative advertising is used by the government, rather than by business organisations, to inform the public about a particular issue – for example, in drink-driving campaigns at Christmas and in health warnings about smoking.

TALK IT OVER

Why do businesses use catchphrases and slogans in their advertising?

TALK IT OVER

What is your favourite advertisement? Why?

Catalogues are a cheaper method of advertising

EEC Council Directive (89/622/EEC)
TOBACCO SERIOUSLY
DAMAGES HEALTH

TOO MUCH PUNCH FOR JUDY.

Persuasive advertising goes further than just giving information. Advertisements are designed to *persuade* the public to buy a given product or service.

In designing advertisements, various tactics are used:

◆ television, film and sports personalities – for example, Gary Lineker in the Walkers crisps advertisements

◆ an appealing story – for example, the Gold Blend advertisements

◆ sex appeal – for example, the Levi Jeans and Renault car advertisements

◆ 'cute' images – for example, the children in the Safeway advertisements, and the Labrador puppy on the Andrex toilet tissue advertisements.

ADVERTISING AGENCIES

Large businesses may employ their *own* advertising team, but many businesses contract **advertising agencies** to do the work for them. The agency plans the complete advertising campaign, including carrying out the market research. This information is then used to develop the campaign. Graphic designers and artists draw up the advertisements, including the graphics and the text to be used. The agency has the advertisements produced, either in printed format or as film footage for a television advertisement, and buys the space in the newspapers or magazines or the time slot on television.

TALK IT OVER

Why might a business employ an advertising agency to produce its advertising campaign?

BUSINESS IN PRACTICE

Halfords' 'We go the extra mile' advertising campaign was a method of promotion aimed at convincing people that the company catered for specialist motor enthusiasts, and did not stock non-specialist products only.

Advertising agency Abbott Mead Vickers produced a series of six advertisements for Halfords, each showing something the company did well. One example was Halfords' rigorous quality-testing; another the innovative car battery with a handle.

The advertisements were shown in Sunday colour supplements, national daily newspapers, television listing magazines and the specialist press.

The campaign strengthened the Halfords brand name and helped to alter customers' perceptions of the company.

Website: www.bized.ac.uk

TALK IT OVER

Why did Halfords use an advertising agency rather than taking on the campaign itself?

Sales promotion is a method of boosting sales or of trying to persuade the customer to try the product for the first time. The most obvious method is an eye-catching point-of-sale display, placed in a prominent place, such as at the entrance to an outlet where these goods are sold.

TYPES OF SALES PROMOTION

Special offers

'Buy one, get one free' (BOGOF) is one type of special offer; another is selling in larger quantities at the same price, such as '25% extra free'. Businesses may offer goods at a reduced price, or even free, if you collect enough tokens or vouchers. For example, a soft-drinks company might offer a free music tape in exchange for 30 ring-pulls.

Free gifts

Businesses may offer free gifts as an enticement to buy the product – for example, some fast-food restaurants give free gifts with their meals. This method has the advantage that the price of the product is not altered. Sometimes cosmetics companies offer a free lipstick if you buy a bottle of perfume or a moisturiser; this too is to get you to try a different product.

Money off

Customers are encouraged to buy the product by getting a reduced price – money off – for buying in large quantities.

Loyalty cards

Loyalty cards are a more recent type of sales promotion. Many supermarkets and retail outlets give their customers loyalty cards: each time they use the store, their purchases gain points or rewards. These are added up and can be exchanged either for cash or for products.

Competitions

Businesses may run competitions, for example offering automatic entry into a holiday prize draw on purchase of a chocolate bar.

INTEREST FREE CREDIT ON ITEMS OVER £300

buy **now** – pay next january

20% DISCOUNT VOUCHER *if you introduce a friend*

Trade promotions

Trade promotions or **trade fairs** are held regularly in large cities all around the world. They are fairs or exhibitions in which businesses selling similar products or services join together under one roof to promote their goods to their customers. These customers are often retailers rather than the general public, although some of the large trade fairs – such as the Clothes Show Live, the Motor Show, and the Ideal Home Exhibition – are also open to the public.

At trade fairs both large and small businesses can rent floor space for a stand, side by side. The exhibition provides a shop window on the particular trade, and businesses can promote, advertise and demonstrate their products.

The Boat Show

BUSINESS IN PRACTICE

Boots The Chemists is very well known for its offers of '3 for 2' and its highly successful Advantage Card loyalty scheme, but it also uses many other methods of promotion.

For example, Boots Opticians launched a fashion voucher promotion with the Arcadia group (Principles, Dorothy Perkins, Top Shop and Burtons): customers who bought designer frames from Boots received a 10% discount voucher for these stores. The promotion was publicised in *Bella*, *Best*, weekend colour supplements and the *Mail on Sunday* to ensure that the target market knew about it.

The messages Boots sent out were, firstly, that spectacles were part of a total image; and, secondly, that if people bought them from Boots Opticians, that image could be achieved at a discount.

The advertising was supported by in-store leaflets, posters, direct-mail campaigns, and competitions in local newspapers.

Website: www.bized.ac.uk

 TALK IT OVER

What was the target market for the Boots Opticians promotion? How could Boots target customers by direct mail?

KEY POINTS

■ **Sales promotions** are used to:
  – boost sales
  – help the launch of a new product.

■ Sales promotions include:
  – special offers
  – free gifts
  – money off
  – loyalty cards
  – competitions
  – trade promotions.

TALK IT OVER

Explain which sales promotions appeal to you.

TEST YOUR UNDERSTANDING

TOPICS 17-23

1 Draw four different channels of distribution.
2 What is the difference between a wholesaler and a retailer?
3 Give three examples of retail outlets and the products sold.
4 Explain what is meant by *network marketing*.
5 What factors must be taken into consideration when choosing a method of transport?
6 List three activities that are part of *promotion*.
7 Why does a business use promotion?
8 Explain the difference between *informative* and *persuasive* advertising.
9 Give two reasons why a business might use an advertising agency.
10 Describe one product that could be advertised: (a) on television; (b) on the radio; (c) in *Yellow Pages*. In each case, give advantages and disadvantages.

CASE STUDY

Coronation Street is the most watched programme on UK television. It has been broadcast since the early 1960s and now reaches more than 15 million households. The UK's favourite soap can be watched 52 weeks per year, four times per week.

When it was announced that broadcast sponsorship was to be permitted, there was a great deal of rumour about which company would sponsor 'The Big One'.

From a list of many possible companies it was Cadbury that successfully struck a £10 million package with Granada (media sales).

The on-air credits, which were created by Bark Films and Aardvark Animation (known for their Wallace and Gromit films), re-created Coronation Street and animated characters in chocolate. In addition to Cadbury's master brand, the Creme Egg, Roses, Time Out and Wispa brands all feature in the credits.

Interactive sales promotions were launched to support the new Cadbury–Coronation Street partnership. Inside the wrapper of Cadbury's bars were numbers and symbols that appeared on the Coronation Street credits.

Both parties are very pleased with the success of the partnership. The sponsorship and promotion have successfully linked two of 'our nation's favourites', and Cadbury has found its way into the homes of millions, giving the business a high profile and a competitive advantage over other confectionery products.

1 Explain the terms: (a) sponsorship; (b) competitive advantage.

2 How would Cadbury benefit from the sponsorship deal?

3 Describe two other methods of promotion used by Cadbury.

4 In its promotion, Cadbury made use of a competition. How can a competition be used successfully to promote a product?

5 The Cadbury master brand and product brands such as Wispa and Roses are well established and well known. What advantage does this bring Cadbury?

EXAM PRACTICE

Tesco supermarkets use regional distribution centres to hold stock. The stock is then taken to local stores using Tesco's own fleet of lorries.

Another more recent change in Tesco's distribution has been to introduce an Internet shopping facility: consumers can order their weekly shopping over the Internet, and it is delivered to their door.

1 Describe carefully how a regional distribution centre operates. [4 marks]

2 What factors should be taken into consideration when a business is choosing a method of transport? [5 marks]

3 Explain why Tesco chose to use road transport to take stock to its stores. [3 marks]

4 Discuss why a consumer might prefer to shop over the Internet rather than visit a Tesco supermarket. [8 marks]

1 Discuss the benefits of a regional distribution centre to a big supermarket chain. [4 marks]

2 What reasons might Tesco have for using road transport to take stock to its local stores? [6 marks]

3 Discuss the advantages and disadvantages of using the Internet: (a) to the consumer; (b) to Tesco. [10 marks]

UNIT 3 Human resources

TOPIC I What motivates people to work?

Businesses are set up to make a profit by providing goods and services to meet consumers' needs and wants. In this unit we start by asking – why do people go to work? What **motivates** them to work?

Providing basic needs

💬 TALK IT OVER

What motivates *you* to work in school?

MOTIVATION

If you asked ten different people what motivates them to work, you would probably get ten different answers. Starting at the most basic level, we all need food, shelter, water, warmth and clothing. To provide these we need money; and to earn money we have to go to work.

Working in a safe environment

Working in a team

Once we have achieved these basic needs, we then begin to have other needs for working. For example:

- Many people need to feel **safe** and **secure** at work – they want to know that they have a job that will pay them a regular wage, a job that offers them a safe working environment, and a job that is secure. Some people still look for a 'job for life', although this is increasingly unrealistic these days. Advances in technology continue to replace jobs which at one time relied on human resources, and at the same time to create new jobs that may need different skills.

Working for power and status

Working creatively

◆ Some people need **friendship** at work or, more importantly, to feel that they are part of a **team**. They enjoy working with other people.

◆ Some people want **self-esteem** from work: they want to feel that they are making a worthwhile contribution.

◆ Some people work to gain the opportunity to **reach their full potential**: they may be **creative** or have certain **skills** that they can use in their job of work.

🗨 TALK IT OVER

What kind of job would give someone self-esteem?

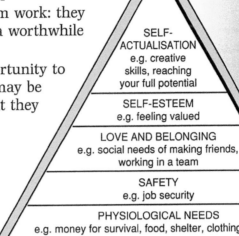

Maslow's hierarchy of needs

MASLOW'S HIERARCHY

The American psychologist Abraham Maslow developed a model of human needs, to show how people are motivated to work.

This model is called a **hierarchy of needs**, because it starts with the basic needs at the bottom and climbs to the higher needs at the top.

There are five levels to the hierarchy of needs. Maslow believed that people start at the bottom of the hierarchy: when they have achieved the first level, such as food and shelter, these needs are no longer as pressing and they become aware of needs at the next level. The reverse is true also: if low-level needs are not being met, high-level needs no longer seem so important. For example, if you are starving, food will probably be the most urgent need.

🗨 TALK IT OVER

Think of a variety of jobs. Which needs might these jobs satisfy?

KEY POINTS

◼ **Motivations** for work include:
- money
- security
- working environment
- friendship
- status
- opportunity to be creative.

◼ **Maslow's hierarchy of needs** is:
- physiological needs
- safety
- love and belonging
- self-esteem
- self-actualisation.

Job satisfaction is the enjoyment a worker gains from doing a job and doing it well. Job satisfaction motivates workers.

Everyone has different needs and wants, so the factors that give a worker job satisfaction will vary.

- Some people are interested only in **money**. As long as the pay is good, they will be happy, even if the job they do is a boring one.

- Other people could not do a boring job. For them to achieve job satisfaction and feel motivated, the job must be **interesting**, and give them **responsibility** and perhaps the possibility of **promotion**.

- Some people are looking for **flexibility**, so that they can combine a family life with a career. Flexible working hours gives them job satisfaction, as such hours allow them to combine work and their personal life.

 TALK IT OVER

What would give *you* job satisfaction?

JOB IMPROVEMENT

Job improvement is the process of making a job more satisfying. This can be achieved in several different ways.

- **Job enlargement** means training workers to carry out a *variety* of jobs. For example, workers on a car production line can be trained to carry out a variety of different tasks. In recent years many car manufacturers have adopted this way of working.

- **Job rotation** is a similar idea. Instead of one worker doing one job all the time, workers move between jobs. This gives each worker a change and a new challenge.

- **Job enrichment** gives workers more responsibility and involvement in the decision-making process for a particular job. Many people like to have the opportunity to prove that they could undertake greater responsibility or be promoted.

Job rotation

◆ **Teamwork** can give job satisfaction – being part of a team and being involved in the decision-making within the team gives the worker a feeling of responsibility and self-esteem. Most people like to 'pull their weight' – to contribute to the work of the team, and not to let the team down.

 **TALK IT OVER**

Would teamwork give *you* satisfaction?

LEADERSHIP STYLES

The ways in which workers are *led* is important – if the workers are not motivated by the leader, the business will not perform as well as it should.

There are three types of leadership style.

Autocratic leadership

The **autocratic leader** makes all the decisions and gives orders to the workers. There is very little communication with the workers. If the leader gives the right orders this style can work well; but it can also be very demotivating for the workers.

Laissez faire leadership

The *laissez faire* **leader** allows workers to 'do their own thing' – to make most of the decisions themselves. This style is good for workers who are confident, but workers may feel that there is no one in charge, and that the business has no sense of direction.

Democratic leadership

The **democratic leader** involves workers in the decision-making. For example, a decision to change working hours will be discussed with workers. This way workers will feel that they have been given the opportunity to influence the decision.

The democratic leader may also **consult** with the workers *before* making decisions. Workers are more involved in decision-making, but it takes much longer to reach decisions.

 **TALK IT OVER**

Which type of leader would *you* prefer?

KEY POINTS

■ Factors that can lead to **job satisfaction** include:
  – fringe benefits
  – possibility of promotion
  – being given responsibility
  – flexible working hours.

■ A job can be made more satisfying by:
  – **enlargement**: giving workers a variety of tasks to do
  – **rotation**: moving teams of workers between different tasks
  – **enrichment**: giving workers more responsibility and greater involvement in making decisions
  – **teamwork**: using teams of workers to increase responsibility and friendship.

■ There are three main **leadership styles**:
  – **autocratic**: workers are told what to do
  – **laissez-faire**: workers are encouraged to make decisions
  – **democratic**: workers are consulted about decisions.

Performance or staff appraisal is used by many businesses. This will involve a review interview between the employee and his or her manager. The interviews are held at regular intervals, usually at least every 12 months.

Appraisals are very similar to the one-to-one reviews held in school between student and teacher, where progress is discussed and targets are set.

STRICTLY PRIVATE and CONFIDENTIAL
APPRAISAL REVIEW

Name *Louie Smith*   Job Title *Assembly worker*   Date *24 April 2001*

SECTION A
Progress made by the job-holder over the last 12 months relative to objectives set earlier
Louie has met two of his objectives:
he has increased the number of components assembled from 75 to 100 per day
he has trained a new employee on the assembly line work

SECTION B
Most important achievements of the job-holder in that period of time
Highest number of components assembled in one day

SECTION C
Barriers the job-holder has experienced that have affected his or her performance
Components not always ready at assembly point on time, slowing down assembly process
Sometimes lacks the ability to communicate problems to Line Manager

SECTION D
Job-holder's strengths
Good timekeeper
Reliable and conscientious worker

SECTION E
Job development and career opportunities
Promote to chargehand when position becomes available

SECTION F
Performance summary
A good worker, well motivated and a good example to other workers

Job-holder's comments
True and accurate review

Job-holder's signature ....   Date ....

Appraiser's signature ....   Date ....

APPRAISAL INTERVIEWS

Before the interview

The employee will be given a **review preparation form**. This gives the employee some points to think about before the interview, in order to prepare for questions the appraiser may ask.

At the interview

◆ The employee and the appraiser – usually the line manager – will talk about the employee's performance at work. They will also discuss future development opportunities, such as further training and promotion.

◆ The employee will then be assessed on his or her performance at work, over a set period of time, and given a rating, together with a brief summary of the interview.

◆ The appraiser will agree new objectives with the employee for the next period of time. Both will then sign a **review document** to record the agreement, and this document will be placed in the employee's file for future reference.

The appraisal process

The appraisal process gives managers an opportunity for one-to-one interviews with employees and helps them to build a better picture of the people working for them. It gives both the manager and the employee the chance to talk about any issues that may have arisen at work during the last appraisal period. It also gives employees a chance to discuss with management future career prospects in the business.

It is important that the employee be set objectives that are achievable, as these will give a sense of purpose and motivation to work harder.

KEY POINTS

Appraisals give:

◼ managers more insight into their employees

◼ managers and employees the chance:
 – to discuss issues and problems
 – to set objectives
 – to discuss future career prospects.

 TALK IT OVER

Should the employee be able to appeal against the appraiser's assessment?

BUSINESS IN PRACTICE

Read the appraisal review on page 104.  **TALK IT OVER**

Is there any training Louie should have?

Pay is the reward for working. It is part of the reason why everybody works. Workers receive either a wage or a salary.

WAGES

Manual or 'blue collar' workers are usually paid weekly wages. These are calculated according to the number of hours worked. The worker is expected to work a certain number of hours – for example, 36 hours per week – and if *more* hours are worked, the worker is paid overtime.

SALARIES

Non-manual or 'white collar' workers, such as office workers, managers and professional people, are usually paid a salary. The hours worked are not fixed, but workers are expected to work a minimum number of hours per week, and often they are expected to stay on at work until their tasks have been completed. A salary is a fixed amount per year, divided into twelve equal monthly payments.

FRINGE BENEFITS

Fringe benefits are any rewards given to workers that do not appear in their pay packet. These benefits are often known as 'perks'. They may include a company car, a company pension scheme, private health care, a subsidised cafeteria, or discounts on goods and services. Fringe benefits are often seen as another way of motivating workers.

PAYSLIPS

When a worker receives a wage or salary, it will be accompanied by a payslip, or pay advice. Payslips show workers their *total* wage or salary (gross pay), the deductions made, and the final amount paid to the worker (net pay).

A The gross pay is the total amount of money earned before any deductions have been made. Gross pay includes extra payments for overtime, and all bonuses.

A manual worker

A 'white collar' worker

TALK IT OVER

Which fringe benefits would *you* like to receive?

Name Patel K			Pay number 7756	Tax code 500H B	NI number HN884523K
Payments			**Deductions**		
Description	Amount £		Description		Amount £
Basic pay Bonus	1800.00 200.00		Income tax Ⓒ National Insurance Ⓒ Pension scheme Ⓓ Trade union Ⓓ		353.61 177.76 90.00 20.00
Gross pay Ⓐ	2000.00		Total deductions		641.37
			Net pay Ⓔ		1358.63

Ⓑ The **tax code** is calculated by the Inland Revenue, and shows how much can be earned before income tax is deducted.

Ⓒ **Statutory deductions** are payments which, by law, *must* be made to the Inland Revenue, on behalf of the government. **Income tax** is money that the government uses to provide services such as education, health, roads and defence. **National Insurance** contributions are used by the government to provide the worker with benefits such as unemployment, sickness and a state pension.

Ⓓ **Voluntary deductions** are payments that workers *choose* to make, for example contributions to a pension scheme, trade union subscriptions, and savings.

Ⓔ **Net pay** is the amount of money received after all deductions – statutory and voluntary – have been made. This is then the worker's take-home pay.

KEY POINTS

■ **Wage** – pay, calculated on an hourly basis.

■ **Salary** – pay, based on an annual figure.

■ The **pay slip** contains information about:
 – **gross pay**: the pay due before deductions
 – **statutory deductions**: paid by all workers
 – **voluntary deductions**: chosen by each worker
 – **net pay**: pay after all deductions.

 BUSINESS IN PRACTICE

After six months service, all employees of Buywise, both full-time and part-time, are entitled to certain benefits. These include a 10% discount on their shopping, a free uniform, and a voluntary pension scheme. Their cafeteria is subsidised.

 TALK IT OVER

How much (in money) might this be worth to an employee?

Different types of payment systems are used to reward workers doing different types of jobs.

OVERTIME

The number of hours a worker is expected to work each week is laid down in the contract of employment. If employees work more hours than those stated, they will be paid an **overtime rate**. This is an extra payment *on top of* the set rate of pay. For example, if a mechanic works overtime, he may be paid $1\frac{1}{2}$ times his normal rate of pay. If the normal rate of pay is £5.00 per hour, the overtime rate would be $1\frac{1}{2}$ times this normal rate – that is, £7.50 per hour.

Calculating bonus

 TALK IT OVER

Why should employees receive a higher rate of pay for working overtime?

PIECE RATES

Workers may be paid according to the number of items they produce, as long as these meet the agreed quality standard. This type of payment usually represents only part of the worker's pay. The worker will receive basic pay *plus* a **piece rate** for meeting a certain target. For example, a worker may be paid extra for each item produced above a target number.

 TALK IT OVER

Why is it necessary to pay a basic wage *plus* piece rate rather than just piece rate?

 TALK IT OVER

What disadvantage could there be with this system?

COMMISSION

A **commission** is paid to workers directly involved in selling services or goods. A car salesperson might be paid 1% of the value of sales made in a month – thus if cars sold had a total value of £50 000, the commission for that month would be £500. As with piece rates, commission is usually paid *in addition* to a basic wage.

Commission is usually paid in addition to a basic wage

PROFIT SHARING

In a profit-sharing scheme workers can use part of their wages to buy shares in the company; this makes them part-owners. The workers may then receive a dividend for investing their wages, as they are now also shareholders. Being a part-owner in the company motivates them to work harder: the more profit the company makes, the higher the dividend they receive. This is also a way for owners to reduce wages and salaries, as well as receiving further investment into the company.

PERFORMANCE-RELATED PAY (PRP)

Performance-related pay is similar to productivity bonuses, but is normally associated with employees whose work cannot easily be measured or attributed solely to them. Members of staff will have targets: if they meet these, they will be paid a bonus. The achievement or non-achievement of targets often forms part of appraisal interviews.

PROFIT-RELATED PAY

Profit-related pay is another additional payment. It is calculated by looking at profit and paying back a proportion of the business's profit to the staff for their contribution to the overall profit.

PRODUCTIVITY BONUS

A productivity bonus is paid to a worker or a group of workers who achieve a set target of output. This encourages workers to produce a higher output in order to achieve the bonus.

KEY POINTS
Wages may be based on:
- a time rate
- a piece rate
- bonus payments
- a profit-sharing scheme.

Salaries may be increased by:
- performance-related pay
- profit-related pay.

TALK IT OVER
What type of jobs would involve PRP?

BUSINESS IN PRACTICE

The John Lewis Partnership refers to its employees as 'partners'. The partners receive an annual bonus which is funded by the company's profits. In March 2001 John Lewis paid a bonus of £58 million, which was equal to 10% of the partners' annual salaries.

 TALK IT OVER
Why might the business operate this bonus scheme?

EQUAL OPPORTUNITIES

An Equal Opportunities policy is a statement drawn up by an employer to ensure that all individuals employed by the business are treated fairly, and that their work is valued irrespective of disability, race, gender, health, social class, sexual preference, marital status, nationality, religion, employment status, age, or membership or non-membership of a trade union.

EQUAL PAY

The Equal Pay Act 1970 requires the employer to pay males and females the same rate of pay for the same job, or for a similar job that has the same demands or the same skill level. This was amended in 1982 to state that work of 'equal value' should receive equal pay.

EMPLOYMENT PROTECTION

The Employment Acts 1980 and 1982 were introduced to give structure to the organisation of industrial relations. These Acts reduced the powers of the trade unions.

SEX DISCRIMINATION

The Sex Discrimination Acts 1975 and 1986 were introduced to ensure that both sexes are treated equally at work. It is illegal for employers to discriminate against men or women in:

- job selection
- terms of employment
- training and staff development
- fringe benefits
- deciding on redundancies.

RACE RELATIONS

The Race Relations Act 1976 makes it illegal for employers to discriminate against people from ethnic minorities.

CONTRACT OF EMPLOYMENT

Under the Employment Rights Act 1996, employers must provide every employee who has been employed for one month or longer with a written statement of working conditions. This must be provided within two months of the employee starting work. The written statement, which must be signed both by the employer and by the employee, includes details of:

- job title
- rate and method of pay
- hours of work
- holiday entitlement
- amount of notice that must be given by employees who wish to leave
- amount of notice that must be given by the employer when dismissing the employee or making the employee redundant
- pension scheme arrangements
- trade union rights
- details of the business's disciplinary procedures
- health and safety at work issues.

 TALK IT OVER

Why is a contract of employment important for employers, as well as for employees?

DISABLED PEOPLE

The **Disabled Persons (Employment) Acts 1944,
1958** and **1981** help disabled people to obtain
employment that best suits their skills. Businesses
have to keep records of disabled employees and to
try to employ a quota of registered disabled people.

HEALTH AND SAFETY

Employers must comply with the **Health and
Safety at Work Act 1974** by drawing up a **health
and safety policy**. This requires *everyone* –
employers and employees – to create a place of work
that is both safe and healthy. The employer agrees to
ensure that all practicable steps are taken to ensure
the health and safety of all employees, and any
other people who may use the business's premises.

All employees are expected to work without risking
their own health or safety, or the health and safety
of anyone else in the business. Employers must
provide suitable training in health and safety at
work, in all aspects that may affect the employee
whilst doing their job, such as:

◆ lifting and handling goods

◆ dealing with waste disposal

◆ using knives and utensils

◆ using machinery and electrical equipment

◆ using ladders.

Employees are obliged to report to the employer any
potentially hazardous situation. They must follow the
guidelines on fire precautions and accident prevention.

Many large businesses issue their employees with a
staff handbook that outlines the business objectives,
the employees' terms and conditions of work, and the
health and safety policy and employees' responsibilities.

KEY POINTS

■ Legislation is used to
protect employees by
ensuring that there is no
discrimination, in terms
of:
– gender
– marital status
– nationality
– ethnic origin
– disability.

■ Employers must
safeguard the health and
safety of their employees.

■ Within two months of the
employee starting work,
the employer must offer a
written statement that
gives all details
concerning employment.

*Employees must not risk their
own health and safety*

BUSINESS IN PRACTICE

Belinda Levez was a betting shop manager for
T. H. Jennings (Harlow Pools) Ltd. Her annual salary was
10% less than that of a male manager. This test case
established the right to claim arrears of pay going back
six years instead of the previous limit of two years.

Adapted from Terrence Shaw: 'Unequal women win
test case on back pay claim', *The Telegraph*, 2.10.99

❞ TALK IT OVER

Consider how this ruling
might affect a range of
different businesses?

TEST YOUR UNDERSTANDING

TOPICS 1–6

1 What is the main reason why people work?
2 Explain the difference between *job enlargement* and *job enrichment*.
3 Describe an autocratic leadership style.
4 Explain the term *appraisal*.
5 Why is it important for employees to be set performance objectives?
6 Distinguish between a *wage* and a *salary*.
7 Explain how *net pay* is calculated.
8 What does the government provide from income tax and National Insurance contributions?
9 Explain the importance of a *contract of employment*.
10 State the responsibilities for safe working of both employers and employees.

CASE STUDY

Clare Hamill is the Vice President of Nike Global Women's Business.

Clare trained originally as an exercise physiologist and worked in a hospital. She first joined Nike as a technician in the Sports Research Laboratories. Since then, she has had a varied career, having been the Product Line Manager for Running Footwear, Director of Product Marketing for Europe, and Vice President for Global Footwear and Nike Equipment.

Clare says that she is looking forward to working with new people and expects that her new work will be fun. Her favourite aspect of working for Nike is meeting one-to-one with the people on her team. She also finds it rewarding to use her own knowledge and experience in her job and enjoys working to push the company on further.

When she is not in the office, Clare enjoys spending time with her 10-year-old daughter. She is a keen runner and also enjoys cycling. Clare believes that helping people or giving them the chance to do great things keeps her motivated each day.

Adapted from an employee profile on the Nike website – www.nikebiz.com/story/b_hamill.shtml

1 Describe what Clare enjoys about her job.
2 What is it that motivates Clare to work hard?
3 Why might Clare have left her job at the hospital?
4 Use Maslow's hierarchy of needs to explain Clare's motivation.
5 What kind of leader do you think Clare might be?

EXAM PRACTICE

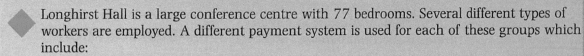

Longhirst Hall is a large conference centre with 77 bedrooms. Several different types of workers are employed. A different payment system is used for each of these groups which include:

– catering and cleaning staff are paid by the hour

– departmental managers (the marketing manager, the finance manager, and the chef) receive a salary

– a performance-related pay scheme is in place for the graphic designer.

All staff are included in the same profit-related bonus scheme.

1 Explain why a time rate was decided upon for the catering and cleaning staff.   [*3 marks*]

2 Why might the catering and cleaning staff prefer being paid by the hour?   [*3 marks*]

3 Describe how a profit-sharing scheme can motivate staff.   [*4 marks*]

4 The graphic designer does not like performance-related pay.
What might be the reason for this?   [*6 marks*]

5 Describe the fringe benefits that the employees might receive.   [*4 marks*]

Longhirst Hall is a large conference centre with 77 bedrooms. Several different types of worker are employed including:

– catering and cleaning staff

– departmental managers (the marketing manager, the finance manager, and the chef)

– a graphic designer.

All staff are included in the same profit-related bonus scheme.

1 Other than performance-related pay, describe the payment system you would use for these employees. Justify your choices.   [*10 marks*]

2 A performance-related pay scheme is in place for the graphic designer, who is unhappy with this. Suggest possible causes for his dislike of this payment system.   [*6 marks*]

3 Why might the business operate a profit-related bonus scheme?   [*4 marks*]

Recruitment is the process of finding people who are best suited to the needs of the business. In a large business, the human resources department will be responsible for recruitment, but this would not be cost-effective in a small business.

JOB ANALYSIS

If a **vacancy** has to be filled, the first stage is a **job analysis**. This identifies the tasks that need to be done and the skills that are required to do them. Sometimes the business needs an exact replacement for someone who has left; but a vacancy also creates the opportunity to change some job descriptions and make the business more efficient.

JOB DESCRIPTION

A **job description** outlines the tasks to be done in that job, and includes details such as:

- the job title
- to whom, and *for* whom, the employee is responsible
- the purpose of the job
- specific duties
- other responsibilities.

PERSON SPECIFICATION

When the job description has been drawn up, a **person specification** is produced. This lists the characteristics of the person needed, such as:

- educational qualifications
- previous experience
- specialised skills
- personal attributes.

RECRUITMENT METHODS

Internal recruitment means looking for suitable applicants from *within* the organisation. Vacancies can be advertised on noticeboards and in company newsletters, or an existing employee may simply be offered the post, often as a promotion.

JOB DESCRIPTION

1 Job title: *Trainee Manager*

2 Responsible to: *Manager*

3 Purpose of job: *Day-to-day running of the shop*

4 Specific duties:
 a) *Staff rotas*
 b) *Staff payroll*
 c) *Keeping financial records*

5 Other responsibilities: *Deputise for Manager*

TALK IT OVER

Why might the business want to change some job descriptions?

PERSON SPECIFICATION

1 Job title:
 Trainee Manager

2 Educational qualifications:
 5 GCSEs at Grade A–C, including Maths and English
 2 A-levels or AVCE*

3 Previous experience:
 *Part-time or work experience
 Retail experience*

4 Personal attributes:
 *Good team member
 Leadership skills
 Good communicator*

5 Specialised skills required:
 Understanding of financial accounts

TALK IT OVER

What would be the benefits of promoting an existing employee?

External recruitment seeks suitable applicants from *outside* the business. Most vacancies are filled in this way. The advantage of external applicants is that they bring new ideas into the business.

Vacancies can be advertised externally:

◆ in local and national newspapers

◆ in specialist magazines – for example, for computer specialists or engineers

◆ on the Internet

◆ in **Job Centres**, which are run by the government

◆ through the **Careers Service**.

A business may also use:

◆ **recruitment agencies**, which charge a fee for providing suitable applicants

◆ government **training schemes**, such as Modern Apprentices

◆ personal recommendation from an existing employee.

PRODUCING A JOB ADVERTISEMENT

A job **advertisement** must:

◆ reflect the job description and the person specification for the job by stating qualifications and experience

◆ be legal with respect to gender and to ethnic and racial minorities.

BUSINESS IN PRACTICE

Many big businesses, such as Sainsbury's, Nike, and Nissan, now include a job opportunities section on their websites.

TALK IT OVER

Why might someone who replied through a website be more suitable than someone who answered an advertisement in a Job Centre?

KEY POINTS

■ **Job analysis** – studying the tasks, skills and qualities involved in a particular job.

■ **Job description** – the tasks and responsibilities of the post and the line manager.

■ **Person specification** – a description of the skills, qualities and experience that the ideal applicant will have.

■ **Recruitment** – involves job analysis, preparing a job description and a person specification, and then advertising the vacancy.

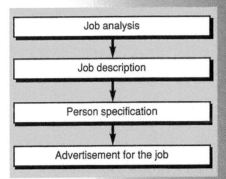

Producing a job advertisement

TALK IT OVER

What types of jobs would be advertised in each of the ways described?

What information should be included in a good job advertisement?

Depending on what the business states in the advertisement, the application process involves either a *letter of application* accompanied by a *curriculum vitae* (CV), or the completion of an *application form*.

CURRICULUM VITAE

The **curriculum vitae** is a document, written by the applicant, which gives details of educational qualifications, past experience, hobbies and interests, and specialist skills.

LETTER OF APPLICATION

A **letter of application** gives applicants the chance to state why they want the job, and why they consider themselves suited to it.

APPLICATION FORM

Many businesses ask applicants to fill in a standard **application form**. This allows the business to ensure that all important information is included, and in an easily accessible format.

SHORTLISTING

After the closing date, applications are considered and a shortlist is drawn up of the applicants who appear to meet the person specification. Remember – the whole purpose of the recruitment procedure is to find the right person for the job.

SELECTION PROCESS

The most common method of selecting new employees for a job is by an **interview**. Other

---

CURRICULUM VITAE

PERSONAL DETAILS

Name: *Yasmin Jeelana*
Address: *22 The Avenue*
                 Shipton
                 Westbridge
                 WA5 7BN

Telephone no.:   *01224 673645*
Marital status: *Single*   Date of birth: *4.5.82*

EDUCATION   *Educated at Westbridge College from 1993 to 2000, including two years in the Sixth Form*

QUALIFICATIONS and TRAINING

GCSEs in English (B), Mathematics (B), History (D), Graphics (B), Business Studies (A), French (C) and PE (D)
A-levels in English Language (D) and Business Studies (D)

PREVIOUS EMPLOYMENT

No previous full-time employment, but have worked weekends and holidays in a local garden centre

HOBBIES and INTERESTS

Enjoy sport and play hockey for a local club
Going out with friends to disco
Interested in embroidery and patchwork sewing

FURTHER DETAILS

Have just passed my driving test
Attending night school to do AVCE in Retailing

Signature .... Date ....

TALK IT OVER

Why might a business prefer applicants to fill in an application form rather than send a CV?

methods of selection which may be used include:

◆ **aptitude tests** of verbal and numerical ability
◆ **personality questionnaires**
◆ a **practical test** – for example, a driving test
◆ **group discussions** and **team-building** and **problem-solving** exercises.

The interview is a face-to-face meeting with an applicant. Each applicant will be asked similar questions, and the responses recorded. Often there will be more than one person on the interview panel.

The interviewer will ask open-ended questions, and interviewees should give reasons for their answers, supported by examples. Examples of questions are:

◆ 'Tell me a little about yourself.'
◆ 'Give me an example of something you did in your previous job which made you proud.'
◆ 'How well do you feel you work as part of a team?'
◆ 'Do you like to work on your own?'
◆ 'What do you see yourself doing in five years' time?'
◆ 'What qualities could you bring to this job?'
◆ 'Why do you want to work for this business?'

Some questions will relate specifically to the job.

MAKING THE APPOINTMENT

The successful applicant will usually be told in writing that she or he is being offered the job, subject to a successful medical examination or **references**.

Once the appointment has been made, the employer and employee will agree a **contract of employment**. The new employee must be issued with a written statement of the terms and conditions of the contract within two months of starting work.

BUSINESS IN PRACTICE

At Alton Towers, the selection process can involve interviews, aptitude tests and group assessments.

TALK IT OVER

Why might Alton Towers use all of these methods?

Bus drivers need to take a driving test before they are taken on as employees

TALK IT OVER

Why are interviews the most popular method of selection?

KEY POINTS

■ The **selection procedure** may include:
  – interviews
  – aptitude tests
  – practical tests
  – personality tests
  – group discussions.
■ Successful applicants must receive a **written statement** of working conditions within two months of starting work.
■ **Reference** – a confidential statement, usually by an employer, outlining a candidate's strengths and weaknesses.

Training is important to a business because it helps to maintain a skilled workforce.

INDUCTION

When new employees start work, they need to find out about the job they are going to do. This introduction to the job may take the form of **induction training**.

In large businesses, induction training may be a structured programme of between one day and one week. New employees may also be given a **staff handbook**. In this are details about:

- the business's objectives
- the employee's terms and conditions of service
- general information about the business, payment systems, training, and trade union membership
- the health and safety policy.

The purpose of the induction programme is to introduce new employees to the job, to help them do the job with confidence and efficiency, and to try to encourage loyalty from new employees.

ON-THE-JOB AND OFF-THE-JOB TRAINING

Employees already working for the business may need training:

- to learn new skills
- to become multiskilled
- to use new technology
- to improve their efficiency
- to help them obtain promotion within the business.

This training may be on-the-job or off-the-job.

On-the-job training is a method of training employees to do a job by putting them to work with an experienced worker. Apprentices learn much of their trade in this way. Trainees in professions such as accountancy or law must first pass their degree, and then have a period of training with a firm before they can become fully qualified.

On-the-job training is often cheap and effective, as

Induction training introduces new employees to a job

 TALK IT OVER

What might be the most important aspect of induction training for a new starter in a call centre?

Apprentices can learn from people who have been doing the job for a long time

long as the experienced worker is efficient. However, the trainee's work may not be of a high standard.

Off-the-job training involves training the employee away from the workplace. This may be at a college or training workshop. Off-the-job training may lead to a qualification such as an A-level, VCE or NVQ. A 'sandwich' course involves spending some time studying, for example at a university, and part of the time working in a business. Some training might be for management or to improve IT skills.

The advantages of off-the-job training are that it is delivered by specialist trainers, and often leads to some form of qualification, which can be useful for future staff development.

Most businesses provide a combination of on-the-job and off-the-job training for employees. Training costs money, both in funding the training and in lost production. Many employers worry that after they have invested time and money in training an employee, the employee may leave the business for a better job, having acquired new skills and qualifications at the business's expense.

A lack of investment in training leads to shortages of skilled workers. More resources are now being provided to improve training, and government-led initiatives such as Investors in People are encouraging employers to invest more time and money in the training of employees.

A business may send employees for training in new work-related skills, or personal skills such as assertiveness

 TALK IT OVER

Would on-the-job training be the most suitable kind of training for a car mechanic?

BUSINESS IN PRACTICE

Kwik-Fit has won many awards for investing in people. It acknowledges that 'people are our most valuable asset'. Developments have included an Outward Bound Team Building programme and a Training Academy for its people.

Website: www.kwikfit.com

 TALK IT OVER

How will these initiatives support the business's slogan: 'You can't get better than a Kwik-Fit fitter'?

 KEY POINTS

- **On-the-job training** – training existing employees as they work.

- **Off-the-job training** – training existing employees outside the company.

- **Induction training** – training employees when they start work, to help them settle in.

RESIGNATION

If an employee wants to **resign** (leave work) voluntarily, perhaps because he or she has found a new job, the employer and the employee must follow the rules laid down in the contract of employment regarding the length of **notice** that must be given.

RETIREMENT

If an employee is about to reach **retirement** age (65), the employer should send the employee a letter confirming the retirement date. Many large businesses now offer retirement seminars to help prepare employees for retirement. If the business has a pension scheme, the employer will help the employee complete the pension application form.

Some employees choose to take **early retirement** from their full-time job. They may then take a part-time job until they receive their pension.

REDUNDANCY

A business may need to make some employees **redundant**. This could be due to a fall in orders, or because automation has been introduced, or because the business wants to reduce capacity ('**downsize**').

If the business does need to make employees redundant, it can begin by asking employees to apply for **voluntary redundancy**. In this case the employee leaves the job in exchange for a cash payment. This is often the first step taken by employers if they need to reduce staff numbers.

If too few employees apply for voluntary redundancy, the next step may be **compulsory redundancy**. In this case the employer ends the contracts of employees whose jobs no longer exist.

The government has introduced legislation to offer some protection to employees who are being made redundant. The business has to make a **minimum redundancy payment** to employees, based on the number of years they have worked for the business.

 TALK IT OVER

What factors might encourage an employee to apply for voluntary redundancy?

TALK IT OVER

Why is voluntary redundancy usually the first step the business takes when reducing staff?

DISMISSAL

An employee can be dismissed for a variety of reasons:

◆ the employee may not be capable of doing the job for which he or she was employed

◆ the employee's conduct may be such that he or she has broken safety rules or endangered other employees' lives through his or her actions

◆ there may be a legal reason why the employee cannot continue in employment – for instance, if he or she is an illegal immigrant.

Employees are protected by the **Employment Protection Act (Consolidation) 1978** against **unfair dismissal**. If they feel they have been dismissed unfairly, they can appeal to an **industrial tribunal**. This is like a court of law: a panel of experts listen to evidence from both the employer and the employee and come to a decision on whether the dismissal was fair or not.

If the tribunal finds that the dismissal was unfair, the business will be required either to **reinstate** the employee or, failing this, to pay the employee **compensation**.

KEY POINTS

◼ **Termination of employment** can be:

– **voluntary**: the employee resigns

– by **retirement**: the employee has reached a certain age

– by **redundancy**: the employee is discharged because the company is abolishing that person's job

– by **dismissal**: the employee is discharged because the company is unhappy with his or her work.

◼ **Downsizing** – reducing the capacity of the business and making the workforce smaller.

BUSINESS IN PRACTICE

Following the takeover of Newshires Cottons by its biggest competitor, Northern Fabrics, Leo Chang and his colleagues were facing the option of uprooting and moving 200 miles north or taking involuntary redundancy and a financial settlement. At first, Leo despaired about the future, but things got better and he found himself having the time of his life doing all the things he had never got round to.

TALK IT OVER

Why do some workers volunteer to be made redundant?

If a business is to succeed, good working relationships between employers and their employees are vital.

INDUSTRIAL RELATIONS

The term **industrial relations** refers to the interaction between the business and its employees. The management of the business will meet with employees' representatives to discuss issues such as:

◆ pay and working hours
◆ equal opportunities
◆ training for employees
◆ production targets
◆ disputes and grievances
◆ health and safety issues in the workplace.

A manual worker – a member of the Transport and General Workers Union (T&GWU)

 TALK IT OVER

What kinds of grievances might workers have?

In a large organisation it is impractical for the employer to talk to each employee individually about issues such as pay or working conditions. Instead the management will meet the representatives of the employees, which might be a trade union or a staff committee.

A white-collar worker – a member of the National Association of Local Government Workers (NALGO)

THE ROLE OF THE TRADE UNION

The main role of a **trade union** is to secure the best possible working conditions for its members, and to promote and protect their interests. It is also much easier for employees if they combine together as a group rather than trying to negotiate pay and conditions individually. This is known as **collective bargaining**.

Other roles for a trade union are to seek training opportunities, and to organise legal representation for any members of the union who feel they have been unfairly treated.

Most trade unions are members of the **Trades Union Congress** (TUC). The TUC cannot tell unions how to run their business, but it does represent the

unions in discussions with the government, trying to influence government policy on a wide range of issues.

EMPLOYERS' ASSOCIATIONS

An **employers' association** is a similar body that represents employers' interests. For example, the Engineering Employers' Federation is an organisation that supports and represents employers in the engineering industry.

Employers' associations:

◆ represent employers in negotiations with trade unions
◆ give employers advice on such matters as training, and health and safety.

The **Confederation of British Industry (CBI)** is a national organisation set up to represent the interests of the employers from all areas of business, in discussions with the government and trade unions.

INDUSTRIAL ACTION

Today employees tend to see themselves as stakeholders in the business and are more likely than in the past to agree on issues with their employers. When agreement cannot be reached, however, an **industrial dispute** occurs.

For example, the employer might argue against a pay rise because recent increases in interest rates have made prices uncompetitive abroad. The trade union might then use some form of **industrial action** to put pressure on the employer. The types of industrial action include:

◆ **work-to-rule** or **go-slow** – the employees go about their work by strictly following the rules that apply to their job: this invariably slows down the production rate
◆ **overtime ban** – the employees work exactly to the hours in their contract of employment and refuse to do any overtime
◆ **boycott** – employees refuse to undertake a particular duty, or to use a particular machine or piece of equipment that the employers are trying to introduce
◆ **strike** – the employees stop working altogether: this may be an **official strike**, if it has been
◆ use a **lock-out**, shutting the premises and stopping the workers from entering to work
◆ stop a previously agreed pay rise.

KEY POINTS

■ **Trade unions** exist to help employees with:
 – disputes over pay and working conditions
 – training
 – health and safety
 – equal opportunities
 – legal representation.

■ **Employers' associations** – associations that help employers in the same way as trade unions help employees.

■ **Collective bargaining** – employees negotiating as a group.

■ **Industrial dispute** – the outcome when discussions between employers and employees fail.

■ **Industrial action** may take these forms:
 – a work-to-rule
 – a refusal to do overtime
 – a boycott
 – a strike
 – a sit-in.

 TALK IT OVER

Why is collective bargaining more effective than individual negotiation?

agreed with their union, or an **unofficial strike**, when employees stop work without the support of the union

◆ **sit-in** – employees occupy the workplace: this approach is often used when a business is threatened with closure, and the employees expect to lose their jobs.

❝❞ TALK IT OVER

How might each of these actions affect a business?

Just as employees in an industrial dispute can take action against employers, so employers can take action against the employees. They can:

◆ threaten to close loss-making parts of the business and make the employees redundant

◆ **sack** workers who refuse to work

◆ **suspend** workers, sending them home without pay for a period of time

Rail pay negotiations break down

Railway workers go on strike

Public pressure grows

Agreement is reached

Commuters can travel again

CONCILIATION AND ARBITRATION

In 1974 a body of people was set up to help employers and employees reach agreement and help them solve their industrial disputes. This body is called the **Advisory, Conciliation and Arbitration Service (ACAS)**. ACAS has representatives from the trade unions and the CBI, and some independent experts on industrial relations.

ACAS can help in the following ways. It can:

◆ meet each side separately, listen to their arguments, and then try to get the employer and the union to meet together – this is called **conciliation**

◆ propose a solution, which neither side has to accept – this is called **mediation**

◆ persuade both sides to agree in advance to accept whatever solution ACAS puts forward – this is called **arbitration**.

KEY POINTS

■ The **Advisory, Conciliation and Arbitration Service (ACAS)** can offer:

– **conciliation**: helping the different sides to discuss a settlement

– **mediation**: suggesting a settlement

– **arbitration**: deciding on a settlement that both sides have agreed to accept.

BUSINESS IN PRACTICE

General Motors experienced a Europe-wide day of protest as workers in Luton and Frankfurt demonstrated against plans to cut thousands of jobs. The president of the German trade union movement said 'The trade union structure in Europe has got to change because of the changing nature of our economies. Cross-border co-operation between unions is the way of the future.'

Adapted from Christine Buckley:
'Unions on the march to a world of
global solidarity', in *The Times*, 26.1.01

 TALK IT OVER

How will businesses be affected if 'cross-border co-operation' becomes a reality?

Agreement reached on new rates of pay

TEST YOUR UNDERSTANDING

TOPICS 7–11

1 Explain the difference between a *job description* and a *person specification*.
2 List four methods of internal recruitment.
3 Discuss what needs to be considered when preparing a job advertisement.
4 Distinguish between *recruitment* and *selection*.
5 What details should be included in a letter of application? Give reasons for your suggestions.
6 Describe what an aptitude test might assess.
7 Using examples, describe off-the-job training.
8 Explain the difference between retirement and redundancy.
9 Discuss the benefits for a business of being a member of an employers' association.
10 Describe three methods of industrial action.

CASE STUDY

When new employees start work at McDonald's they receive induction training. This introduces them to the company and to the restaurant where they will be working. During the induction training there is a tour of the restaurant, an opportunity to complete tax forms, and a test on health and safety and hygiene. After this follows a three-week probationary period before a performance review is conducted.

There are 16 areas in which the employee must be proficient. This will take four months for a full-time member of staff, and about eight months for a part-time employee.

McDonald's operates a 'buddy' system. Every new employee is given a 'buddy' who will be a mentor and help the employee through the training. The employee's buddy carries out each stage of the assessment. The pass mark for these tests is 90%!

After training an employee has a pay review twice a year, at which the employee's performance is assessed and further training discussed.

The career structure in McDonald's is excellent. 80% of top managers started as 'crew members', which is what the restaurant teams are called. This is the proof that the McDonald's training programmes are effective.

1 Explain why induction training is important both for the employees and for the business.

2 Suggest why the new employee has a test on health and safety and hygiene so soon.

3 McDonald's has a three-week probationary period. Why might this be?

4 Explain why the fact that 80% of managers started as crew members is proof of an effective training programme.

5 Evaluate the 'buddy' system.

EXAM PRACTICE

BLAST is a small but very successful business which produces computer games. The business is so successful that a computer programmer and a sales manager need to be appointed.

◆ 1 Identify suitable methods of recruitment for: (a) the computer programmer; (b) the sales manager. [4 marks]

2 What method of selection would you advise for the computer programmer? [2 marks]

3 Design a person specification for the sales manager, and give reasons for your suggestions. [6 marks]

4 Discuss the training that will be needed for: (a) the computer programmer; (b) the sales manager. [8 marks]

◆ 1 Discuss the methods of recruitment that would be suitable for these two positions. Advise BLAST on the most appropriate methods. Justify your choices. [12 marks]

2 Design a training programme for the two new employees. [8 marks]

The importance of communication

Good **communication** is essential if a business is to succeed. Businesses need to communicate to gather information, to give information, and to discuss issues.

WHAT IS GOOD COMMUNICATION?

Communication occurs when a **sender** transmits a message using a suitable **medium** to a **receiver**. Communication is known to have been effective when the receiver gives the sender **feedback** which shows that the message has been understood and, if appropriate, acted upon.

An example of communication is a manager asking a worker to order some stock. Good communication would be evident if the worker ordered the stock and gave feedback to the manager about when the stock would be delivered.

 TALK IT OVER
Discuss examples of good communication.

Informal communication

INTERNAL AND EXTERNAL COMMUNICATIONS

Internal communication takes place between people *inside* the business. Examples of internal communications include:

- a manager sending a memorandum to remind supervisors of a meeting
- an accountant sending an e-mail to the sales manager
- an advertisement on a noticeboard for an internal vacancy.

External communication takes place between the business and *outside* organisations and people, such as other businesses, customers or the Inland Revenue.

BARRIERS TO COMMUNICATION

There will be a **breakdown in communication** if something goes wrong with the important elements of the communication process.

MEMO

From: Production Manager
To: Production Supervisors
Subject: Flexitime arrangements
Date: 27 April 2001

Following a meeting of all Heads of Department with Human Resources, it has been decided to change the core hours that employees must report for duty to 10.00am to midday and 2.00pm to 4.00pm. These changes will take effect from 1 May 2001. Please can you therefore ensure that you notify all relevant staff of these changes.

Formal communication

- The *sender* might send a long or confusing message, or accompany it with inappropriate body language, or even send it to the wrong person.
- The *medium* might be unsuitable – there might be too many people involved (like 'Chinese whispers'), or the telephone, fax or computer might break down, or a complicated message might be sent verbally instead of being written down.
- The *receiver* might not read or listen carefully, or might not understand the language used, or might just decide to ignore the message.
- The *feedback* might be confusing and ambiguous, or might not be given at all.

 TALK IT OVER

Have you any experience of a breakdown in communication? How did it happen?

CHANNELS OF COMMUNICATION

When a message passes from one person to another, it travels along **channels of communication**. These may be *formal* (*vertical* or *horizontal*) or *informal*.

Formal channels of communication are agreed by the management and workers. They can be vertical or horizontal – **vertical communications** pass up and down the hierarchy; **horizontal communications** pass along at the same level of the hierarchy.

Informal communications are the chat and gossip that occur between workers. They are often called the '**grapevine**'. Informal communications follow no set route – information can be passed on to anyone who is listening.

BUSINESS IN PRACTICE

A study by the Industrial Society claims that 'gossip is the cement which holds organisations together and is crucial to their performance'.

Adapted from Elizabeth Judge: 'Gossiping at work is "good for companies"', in *The Times*, 22.11.00

 TALK IT OVER

Do you think that the 'grapevine' is always as productive as the report suggests?

KEY POINTS

- **Communication** can be:
  - **internal**: between people inside the business
  - **external**: between the business and people outside it.
- A **message** travels:
  - from a **sender**
  - to a **receiver**
  - using a particular **medium** (method of communication)
  - the receiver lets the sender know that the message has been understood by giving **feedback**.
- **Formal communications** use a structured medium of communication, recognised and accepted by everyone in the business, e.g. noticeboards or e-mail.
- **Informal communications** are the gossip and rumours passed around the business, often called the '**grapevine**'.
- **Vertical communication** involves information being passed up or down the hierarchy.
- **Horizontal communication** involves information being passed between people on the same level in a hierarchy.

METHODS OF COMMUNICATING

There are four methods of communication – *non-verbal*, *verbal*, *written* and *visual*.

Non-verbal communication is the body language we use when we are with people. For example, we might nod our heads in agreement, or shake our heads in disagreement. Body language is often used to emphasise verbal communications – for example, a manager might smile when praising a worker, or frown when correcting another.

Verbal communication involves talking with people. Examples include interviews, meetings, telephone conversations and video-conferencing.

Written communications are useful because they can be referred to at a later date. Examples include letters, reports, minutes, notices, newsletters, faxes, and e-mails; business documents such as invoices and memoranda; and electronic data such as databases.

Visual communications are designed to give information quickly and with an impact. Examples include posters, charts and diagrams, and films and videos.

BUSINESS COMMUNICATIONS

The main methods of communication used by businesses are listed in the table opposite. The method chosen will depend upon the situation, cost,

Verbal communication

Delta Plastics International

23 Woodlands Road, Leeds, LS4 2J0

The Sandwich Box	VAT Reg 456 543
Unit 28	Invoice no 4765
Penraven Industrial Estate	Date 30/11/00
Mean Wood Road	
Leeds	
LS7 2AP	

INVOICE

100 plastic cartons (small)	£50.00
100 plastic cartons (medium)	£70.00
100 plastic cartons (large)	£95.00
Subtotal	£215.00
Plus VAT (17.5%)	£37.62
Total Due	£252.62
E&OE	

Written communication

Non-verbal communication should be appropriate to the situation

Method	Advantages	Disadvantages
Verbal	Instant communication Immediate feedback	No written record May take a long time Prone to interference by noise
Written	Written record for future reference Can be reproduced	Presentation may cause disinterest in the receiver Feedback takes time
Visual	Can catch the attention of the receiver No language barrier Can emphasise points effectively	There may be no direct feedback Could be ambiguous Interpretation of information may require certain skills
Electronic	Instant communication Immediate feedback possible A large amount of information can be handled easily	Equipment may be expensive Equipment may break down Not all businesses have suitable equipment

and time available. For example, a contract might be faxed to someone so that they could read through it immediately, but the original would be sent by post so that it could be signed.

E-commerce

E-commerce is the term used to describe buying and selling over the **Internet**. Businesses can now use their own websites to tell customers about the business and what they offer, and to advertise their products. Customers can order goods over the Internet, using their credit or debit cards.

For many small businesses this has created opportunities to beat the competition, but in early trading many businesses failed due both to a lack of capital and cash-flow problems.

BUSINESS IN PRACTICE

A sales representative, speaking on the telephone, might finish the conversation by saying, 'Thank you for your order. Please confirm it in writing.'

TALK IT OVER

Why would the telephone order need to be confirmed in writing?

KEY POINTS

■ **Non-verbal communication** – using body language to communicate.

■ **Verbal communication** – communicating by talking.

■ **Written communication** – recording messages in writing.

■ **Visual communication** – communicating using posters, charts, diagrams, films and videos.

■ **E-commerce** – buying and selling using the Internet.

MEMORANDUM

A **memorandum** (usually called a **memo**) is a short note sent from one person to another *within* a business. It is used when it is necessary to keep a record of the information being sent.

The example (on page 128) shows the headings that are generally used.

ELECTRONIC MAIL

As **electronic communication** becomes more popular, the paper memo is becoming a thing of the past. Now employees within an organisation are more likely to send each other an electronic mail message – an **e-mail**.

BUSINESS LETTERS

A business **letter** is probably the most common type of external communication, although it is fast being replaced by e-mails and faxes.

REPORTS

Reports need a clear structure.

◆ There should be a **title page** which includes the business name, a clear title for the report, and the **terms of reference**, which state the objectives and purpose of the report.

◆ The **introduction** should set the scene and explain clearly what the report is about.

◆ The **findings** or **content** will present any results in readable style.

◆ The **conclusion** summarises the findings or content, and states

---

To: Judy Piotrowski <judy.piotrowski@traxtours.com>
Sent: 10 April 2001 14:06
From: Rachida Shah <rachida.shah@traxtours.com>
Subject: Vision Car Hire

Dear Judy
Mr and Mrs Collinson came into the shop today and complained about the extra charges Vision Car Hire put on their bill - despite their thinking everything was pre-paid. I have asked them to put their complaint in writing.

This is the third complaint about Vision Car Hire this month and I am concerned that our tailor-made packages will get a bad name.

Rachida

J & J Clothing

2 Newtown Industrial Estate, Newtown NI6 5AB
Tel: 01112 222111   Fax: 01112 112211

Mr P Rayner
Customer Services Manager
Material Supplies
22 Park Road
BRIDGETOWN
OP2 5AB

3 May 2001

Dear Mr Rayner

Polyester delivery – Order no: 32789

It has been brought to my attention that the above order has not yet been delivered. The order was placed on 19 January 2001. My assistant has telephoned your department on four different occasions and has been told each time that the order is on its way.

I would be grateful if you would let me know as soon as possible when the order will arrive, and explain the delay.

Yours sincerely

Ms H Aitcheson
Production Director

what these mean in relation to the terms of reference.

◆ **Recommendations** are made at the end of the report which make positive suggestions for future action.

 TALK IT OVER

Suggest different occasions when a large firm, such as Nissan, would use these types of business document.

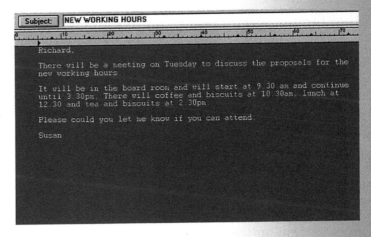

Subject: **NEW WORKING HOURS**

Richard,

There will be a meeting on Tuesday to discuss the proposals for the new working hours.

It will be in the board room and will start at 9.30 am and continue until 3.30pm. There will coffee and biscuits at 10.30am, lunch at 12.30 and tea and biscuits at 2.30pm.

Please could you let me know if you can attend.

Susan

RAPID TRAVEL

REPORT ON VISION CAR HIRE

19/4/01

Terms of reference

To investigate complaints that have been received about extra charges from Vision Car Hire, and to consider whether it is in the company's best interests to continue using this firm.

Introduction

There have now been ten complaints about extra charges being levied by Vision Car Hire. We state in our tailor-made package brochure that the car hire is pre-paid.

Findings

The complaints
Three couples were charged £25 for 'post-trip maintenance', two couples have been charged £30 for 'fuel missing', and five people have been charged £20 for 'post-trip cleaning'.

Response from Vision Car Hire
The 'fuel missing' charge is, apparently, standard if a car is brought back without a full tank of petrol. However, Vision have admitted that the 'post-trip maintenance' and 'post-trip cleaning' should not have been charged as they are included in the price we pay them as part of the deal. They have agreed

2

to refund the money they have received for those charges, and assured us that such charges will not be made again.

Figures
The tailor-made packages form a large part of our business – 20% – and the inclusion of car hire in the deal is particularly popular (75% of customers say that it is important for them). The deal with Vision is a good one and they also market our business as part of the deal by distributing leaflets to their customers.

Conclusion

We cannot afford to lose customers through Vision Hire's extra charges. The car hire is important as these packages form 20% of our business and most customers say it is important to them. The association with Vision Hire is of benefit to us as they perform a marketing function for us.

3

Recommendations

I propose that we continue with Vision for the time being, and monitor their service carefully. At the same time, we should investigate alternative car hire companies in case we need to change in the future.

We should put a statement in the letter that is sent to customers with their tickets, informing them that they are required to return the car with a full tank of petrol, otherwise a charge of £30 will be levied by the car hire company.

Providing we monitor them carefully, I believe that we should be able to continue our relationship with Vision satisfactorily.

4

KEY POINTS

■ **Memorandum** – a note sent within a business.

■ **E-mail** – rapid communication using computer systems.

■ **Business letter** – the most common form of written communication.

■ **Report** – a clearly structured document that presents findings from research, draws conclusions, and makes recommendations.

UNIT 4 Production

TOPIC I — Production decisions

Production is the process of using **resources** and **adding value** to them, to make a **product** or provide a **service** that consumers will want to buy.

PRODUCTION PROCESS

When producing a good or providing a service, production involves processing **inputs** to produce an **output**: *input → process → output*. The inputs of **factors of production** are combined or processed to produce the output of a good or service.

PRODUCTION DECISIONS

Managers in charge of producing goods or services need to make decisions about:
- what to produce
- how to produce it
- where to produce it.

These managers will also need to make sure that the business produces:
- the right quantities
- at the right price
- and of the right quality.

THE PRODUCT

The production managers will find out from the marketing department what the consumers want, and what other businesses – the **competition** – are producing. No single part of a business operates on its own: all departments must work together to make the product successful.

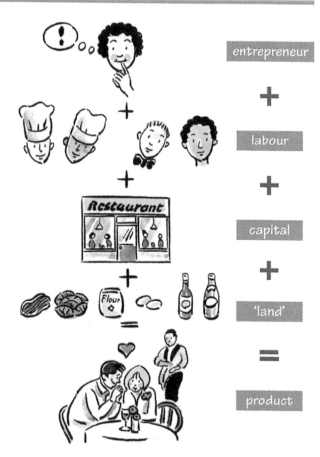

entrepreneur

+

labour

+

capital

+

'land'

=

product

 TALK IT OVER

Choose a variety of products and identify the inputs for each.

 TALK IT OVER

Why does the production department need to have contact with the marketing, finance and human resources departments?

THE PRODUCTION PROCESS

The production managers will choose each production process carefully, as their choice will affect how much profit is made. Most production will depend upon machines and **automation**: manufactured goods are produced in this way. Some production will tend to use a greater amount of **labour**: examples include house-building and services such as retailing.

The **location** of production is affected by the type of product being made – for instance, perishable goods such as bread and bakery products are usually produced near to where they will be sold.

THE FINAL PRODUCT

The production department needs to produce just the right **quantity** of goods. Producing too many goods, known as **over-production**, may cause financial problems for the business: capital would be tied up in the unsold stock, and this could cause **cash-flow problems** (see Unit 5, Topic 2). Over-production of perishable goods would mean that stock might have to be destroyed, which could cause a loss for the business.

Not producing enough goods will also cause problems for the business. If customers do not receive their orders, or have to wait too long for deliveries, the business may lose those customers to rival producers.

The business must decide the best **price** for its goods. The price must be one that customers are able and prepared to pay, but which still allows the business to make a profit. The price will be affected by various factors (see Unit 2, Topics 14–16), including the cost of production. The cost of production will, in turn, be affected by the quality of the final product, which must meet the customers' needs. For example, there is no point in a business producing football shirts of such a high quality that the materials used make the shirts too expensive for customers to buy.

TALK IT OVER

How can the production department find out about the quantity of goods to supply?

KEY POINTS

- **Production** – combining the **factors of production** to produce **goods** and **services**.

- Production decisions include:
  - what to produce
  - how to produce it
  - where to produce it.

- The main objectives of the production department are:
  - right product
  - correct quantity
  - right price
  - efficient methods
  - product quality.

TALK IT OVER

How might the cost of production be affected by the quality of the final product?

An objective of the production department is to produce goods as **efficiently** as possible. This requires that the costs of production be kept as low as possible, without affecting the quality of the goods and services produced.

Different combinations of labour and capital will affect the efficiency of the production process.

Labour-intensive production

EFFICIENCY IN THE PRODUCTION OF GOODS

Some methods of production use large quantities of labour compared to capital: people, rather than machines, do most of the work. This is called **labour-intensive production**. Other productive processes rely heavily on machinery, and employ very few workers. This is called **capital-intensive production**.

The choice of production process will depend upon:
◆ the nature of the product
◆ the availability of technology
◆ the scale of production.

Capital-intensive production

THE NATURE OF THE PRODUCT

An example of the difference in approaches is the Morgan sports car. Morgan still uses traditional labour-intensive methods for building cars. Each car is hand-built, and people who wish to buy a new Morgan face a six-year wait. They accept this because they like the fact that the Morgan is different from other cars.

By contrast, Ford builds cars on an automated production line, using all the latest technology. Customers could order a new car and would probably take delivery of it within a few weeks. However, a Ford car does not have the features of a Morgan.

 TALK IT OVER

Can you think of any other products that consumers buy because they have been 'hand-made'?

Morgan body shop

AVAILABILITY OF TECHNOLOGY

The service sector must also aim for maximum efficiency, if costs are to be kept as low as possible. It used to be the case that the production of services relied almost totally on labour and very little on capital. As technology has advanced, however, businesses that produce services have introduced more automation, and reduced the proportion of labour.

Examples of technology being used to improve efficiency and to reduce the costs of production can be found in banking and other financial services, in retailing, in transport, and in travel. The banks' introduction of cash machines and telephone and Internet banking has resulted in their being criticised for closing branches and 'losing the personal touch'.

In some instances, **methods of working** have been adapted to increase efficiency. For example, not only have supermarkets introduced computerised systems for stock and sales, but they also train checkout operators in how to pass goods over the barcode readers as quickly and accurately as possible.

SCALE OF PRODUCTION

Increased efficiency can sometimes be achieved through the organisation of the production process. For example, a production line might be divided into a series of tasks, with workers at the different stages specialising in different tasks. The result is that goods can be produced more quickly. This process, based on **division of labour**, made **mass production** possible.

When goods are produced on a large scale, the average cost of producing the goods can be reduced. For example, if raw materials are ordered in large quantities, their supplier might give a **discount** that would not be given for a small order. Such savings are called **internal economies of scale** (see Unit 4, Topic 9).

 TALK IT OVER

Why might a supplier give discounts on *large* orders, but not *small* orders?

KEY POINTS

- **Productive efficiency** – methods of production that keep the costs of producing goods to the minimum.

- **Automation** – using computer-controlled machinery, thereby reducing the need for workers.

- **Division of labour** – breaking the production process into smaller stages, allowing workers to concentrate on particular tasks.

- **Internal economy of scale** – a reduction in the average cost of production as a result of producing goods on a large scale.

To increase efficiency, supermarkets train checkout operators to scan items quickly and accurately

Production managers must choose the best methods to use in producing their goods.

There are three main methods:

◆ produce each item individually (**job production**)

◆ produce items in batches (**batch production**)

◆ produce items continuously (**flow production**).

In choosing between them, the manager will consider:

◆ the **cost of production** for each method

◆ **how many** products the business wants to make

◆ which method produces the **best-quality** product.

Job production

JOB PRODUCTION

Job production is when each product is made individually, to meet each customer's specific order. Each order is likely to be different, so batch or flow methods are unsuitable.

Job production often involves skilled labour or craftspeople. It is **labour-intensive**, relying heavily on labour rather than machinery. The emphasis is *quality*, not quantity. Goods made by job production are often very expensive, as there are few economies of scale.

This method of production is suited to items such as made-to-measure clothing. Large items, as well as small ones, may be individually made. An example is boat-building, in which clients may want their boat fitted out to their personal requirements.

Batch production

BATCH PRODUCTION

Batch production is used to produce a number of similar products – a **batch**. When that order has been completed, another batch is produced. For example, clothes manufacturers use batch production to produce a given item, such as a jacket, in batches of different sizes or colours.

Batch production allows the producer to be flexible, and to produce a range of similar goods which meet the needs of different customers.

Flow production

 TALK IT OVER

Clothes can be made using either job or batch methods of production. What will influence the producer when choosing the production method?

FLOW PRODUCTION

Flow production is a capital-intensive process in which products move continuously along a **production line** through different stages of production. For example, production of a car will start with the shell at the beginning of the production line, with various parts being added as the shell moves along the line. This process of breaking down production into stages is known as **division of labour**.

Flow production allows large numbers of fairly standard products, such as computers, oil or food, to be produced quickly, and is sometimes referred to as **mass production**.

BUSINESS IN PRACTICE

Greggs plc is the UK's leading retailer specialising in bakery products, which are produced for the shops in Greggs' own bakeries. Bread, rolls, savouries and cakes are produced using the batch method of production. Production lines are semi-automated, and the workers are semi-skilled.

Greggs also makes speciality cakes for occasions such as weddings, birthdays, and charity events. Workers skilled in cake decorating use job production for these special cakes, which are made to customers' specifications.

Warburton's is the third largest brand of bakery goods in the UK. Unlike Greggs, Warburton's uses flow production for its fully automated white-bread production line.

TALK IT OVER

Why have these bakeries chosen to use different methods?

KEY POINTS

- The three main methods of producing goods are:
  - **job production**: making products individually, to order
  - **batch production**: making sets of similar products
  - **flow production**: making products continuously on a **production line**.

- Using job production:
  - needs a skilled workforce
  - is labour-intensive
  - has a high cost of production.

- Using batch or flow production:
  - allows large quantities to be made
  - is capital-intensive
  - allows economies of scale.

- **Division of labour** – breaking the production process into stages, with workers specialising in particular tasks.

Much of the success of Japanese manufacturers is due to their developments in the process of mass production, which have cut the costs of production and increased the rate and quality of output.

Toyota was the first manufacturer to introduce **lean production**. This uses a range of techniques to reduce waste and to use the minimum number of workers and amount of resources in production. All employees are expected to be committed to *kaizen* – Japanese for **continuous improvement** – and they are encouraged to think continually about ways to improve the products and the production process.

Lean production involves introducing new techniques and methods into the production process.

IMPROVING WORKERS' PRODUCTIVITY

Usually, workers are grouped into teams, each with responsibility for a certain part of the production process. This is known as **team-working**. Workers are trained to do a range of tasks, and become **multiskilled**. They also receive training to improve their team skills. The workers have authority to make decisions relating to their own work – they are said to be **empowered**.

Some producers have introduced **cell production**. Instead of each team concentrating on *part* of the production line, a team of workers, working as a cell on a 'mini-production line', completes the *whole* process. This approach uses much less factory space than a long production line. Cell production may even involve the team working right through from design of the product to dealing with customers.

Workers may also be involved in **quality circles**. These are groups of employees who are encouraged to discuss ways of solving problems and to make suggestions for continuous improvement.

The increased training and responsibility that go with such approaches encourage workers to feel trusted, and they are more highly motivated than workers on a traditional production line.

Team-working

 **TALK IT OVER**

Why might the introduction of team-working *demotivate* some workers?

USING RESOURCES MORE EFFICIENTLY

Just-in-time (JIT) production uses stocks that are delivered to the production line 'just in time' to be used. With this approach, the business needs less factory space, as it holds smaller stocks; but it depends on suppliers agreeing to meet delivery requirements. The business does not have so much money tied up in stock or warehousing costs. However, the reliability of the supplier in delivering good-quality stock on time is crucial to keeping the production process running smoothly.

TALK IT OVER

What kind of problems might arise as a result of introducing JIT?

KEY POINTS

- **Lean production** aims to reduce waste in the production process and to increase the productivity of workers.

- **Continuous improvement** is achieved because workers are more motivated as a result of the introduction of team-working, empowerment, multiskilling, and increased training.

- **Suppliers** have a greater influence in the success of the business when lean production techniques and methods are introduced.

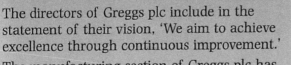

BUSINESS IN PRACTICE

The directors of Greggs plc include in the statement of their vision, 'We aim to achieve excellence through continuous improvement.'

The manufacturing section of Greggs plc has always supplied the Greggs retail outlets, so just-in-time deliveries have been a feature of the business for many years. This is an aspect of JIT which superstores such as Sainsbury's and Tesco have introduced in recent years. These stores, like the Greggs shops, have no space for stock and are totally dependent on JIT deliveries to meet the needs of the customers.

TALK IT OVER

Do you think just-in-time deliveries have improved service for the consumer?

REVIEW 1

TEST YOUR UNDERSTANDING

TOPICS 1–4

1 Describe the decisions that a production manager needs to make.
2 What is meant by the *production process*?
3 What are the four *factors of production*?
4 What is *productive efficiency*?
5 Explain how technology has improved efficiency.
6 What is *mass production*?
7 Explain the difference between *job production* and *batch production*.
8 How does batch production allow the manufacturer to be more flexible?
9 What is meant by *cell production*?
10 Explain the purpose of introducing *lean production*.

CASE STUDY

Many estate agents now have websites which show prospective buyers a range of properties.

Keith Pattinson Estate Agents are the North East's largest independent estate agent. Their aims state:

'As a company we are focused on innovation. We aim to offer the most efficient service possible to our clients.'

FPDSavills is a much bigger organisation than Keith Pattinson, and is one of the world's major providers of integrated global property services. The business makes extensive use of technology, and details of the wide range of services offered can be found on its website (www.fpdsavills.co.uk).

Presumably FPDSavills is also committed to providing an efficient service so why, in the age of the virtual property tour, does it still produce glossy property brochures, given it also lists the property on its website?

Such brochures can cost £250 for a standard house and up to £13 000 for more sophisticated estates. Typically they include

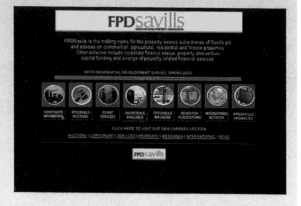

lots of photographs, room plans, a map of the surrounding area, and views from the house.

Producing a brochure is labour-intensive and very time-consuming. The photographers must show the house at its most attractive, and the date on which the photographs were taken must be displayed.

In this age of the 360-degree virtual-reality tours of property, these very expensive glossy brochures seem out of place.

Adapted from Gwenda Brophy: 'Era of glossy images lives on', in *Financial Times*, 27.1.01

1 What services do estate agents provide for their clients?

2 Why might Keith Pattinson Estate Agents value innovation?

3 How can using the Internet improve the efficiency of the service offered by estate agents?

4 What are the advantages and disadvantages of using the Internet to show properties?

5 Why might glossy property brochures still be produced?

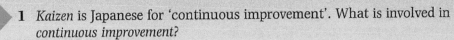

EXAM PRACTICE

1 *Kaizen* is Japanese for 'continuous improvement'. What is involved in *continuous improvement?* [3 marks]

2 Explain how a clothing manufacturer could introduce the following into the business: (a) team-working; (b) quality circles; (c) just-in-time. [9 marks]

3 Discuss the effects on the workers of introducing new methods of working. [8 marks]

1 Explain how a clothing manufacturer could introduce 'continuous improvement' into the production process. [8 marks]

2 Discuss the effects on workers' motivation of new methods of working. [12 marks]

All types of business must control **stock levels** to make sure that there is the right amount of stock to meet the needs of their customers. Manufacturers need to hold enough stocks of raw materials and components to keep the production line working, so that they can meet customers' orders. The service sector too requires a range of stocks – for example, hairdressers need hair products, garages need petrol and spare parts, and restaurants need food and wine. If a business runs out of stock, its customers may turn to its competitors.

The business also needs to make sure that there is not *too much* stock on the premises: if there is, it may deteriorate or be damaged. **Overstocking** – holding too much stock – means that money is tied up in goods: this is inefficient and could cause cash-flow problems (see Unit 5, Topic 2).

TALK IT OVER

Is it necessary for a business to monitor every single line of stock that it uses?

Manufacturers need to hold enough stocks of raw materials to keep the production line working to meet the customers' orders

STOCK LEVELS

To prevent too little stock being held, the production manager will fix a *minimum* stock level and a *re-order* stock level, for each item of stock.

The **minimum stock level** is the least amount of stock needed to keep the business running. However, it would not be sensible to allow stock to fall to the minimum level before ordering, because deliveries take time to arrive from suppliers. This is known as the **lead time**. A **re-order level** is therefore set, to allow for this time between placing an order and the order being delivered.

The **maximum stock level** is set to keep the costs of holding stock as low as possible. This level will depend on the amount of storage space available, on whether the stock is perishable, fashionable or seasonal, and on the amount of money tied up. When deciding upon the maximum level, the business will also need to consider the stock needed to meet sudden increases in orders.

Many large stores monitor stock levels electronically. The electronic point of sale (EPOS) at the checkout scans bar codes and stock levels are updated automatically.

KEY POINTS

- **Understocking** – not holding enough stock, which may lead to lost customers.

- **Overstocking** – holding too much stock, which may lead to lost profit.

- **Stock control** – managing stock levels so that the business has enough stock to meet customers' needs, but not so much that there is inefficiency.

MANAGING STOCK LEVELS

The graph shows how the stock levels of components can be managed.

- The maximum amount of components that can be be held in the warehouse is 700 boxes.

- Production would stop if stocks fell below 200 boxes.

- The suppliers of the components take 6 days to deliver after having received the order, so the re-order level is set at 400 boxes.

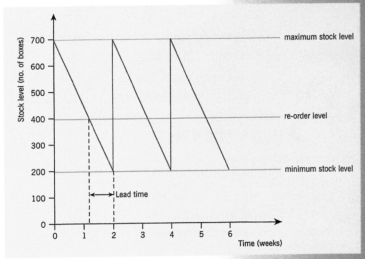

TALK IT OVER

How can producers of seasonal goods manage stock levels?

Businesses realise the importance of meeting their customers' needs and wants by providing them with a product that meets the standard expected by the customer.

QUALITY CONTROL

With **quality control**, goods may be tested at various stages of the production process.

The first step is to check the *raw materials* or *components* coming from the suppliers. If a just-in-time system is in place (see Unit 4, Topic 4), the supplier is expected to test the products, and to guarantee that they are free from defects before delivering them.

The next step is to check the *work in progress*. This means taking **random samples** of the products at suitable stages of the production process, and checking the quality of the work and of the product.

The final step is to check the *finished product*. Any faulty goods are taken out and scrapped.

Quality control can be expensive, as there can be a lot of waste if a batch of products is found to be faulty. Errors can arise from:

◆ workers not paying attention and making mistakes
◆ faulty raw materials and components
◆ machinery breaking down
◆ design faults going undetected into production.

QUALITY ASSURANCE

Quality assurance is provided when the business *guarantees* the quality of a product to its customers. The business can guarantee quality by working to independent **quality standards** such as those of the **British Standards Institution** (**BSI**). By displaying the BSI kitemark on its products – for example, motorcycle helmets – the business is claiming that those products meet the BSI standards.

Other **quality marks** include the **CE mark**, which is recognised throughout the European Union (EU), and the logo of the Association of British Travel Agents (ABTA).

The BSI kitemark and the CE safety mark

TALK IT OVER

How many quality marks can you think of?

The business may also offer customers a **warranty** – a statement that for a stated period of time after the customer has bought the product, any faults will be put right free of charge.

TOTAL QUALITY MANAGEMENT

Total quality management (TQM) requires *everyone* in the business to think about *quality* – not only the production teams, but also all the other employees in the business. All employees are encouraged to make suggestions for improving the standard of their work. By taking this approach, TQM makes quality management part of the production process. Employees aim to eliminate mistakes and shoddy work, and this cuts costs and wastage. Employees take a pride in their work, and the customer receives a quality product.

TQM introduces **quality circles**, which are small groups of workers who meet regularly to discuss their work problems and to find solutions. A quality circle may be set up to solve a particular problem or to focus on general issues. The purpose of quality circles is to motivate the workers and improve efficiency; the workers are likely to be more responsive if they are involved in overseeing the production process.

TALK IT OVER

How might TQM improve a worker's job satisfaction?

 **KEY POINTS**

- **Quality control** – checking the product at various stages during production.
- **Quality circles** – groups of workers discussing how to improve their work and to solve any production problems.
- **Warranties** – issued to the customer by the producer, to give quality assurance.
- **Total quality management** – encouraging all employees to consider the quality of their work.

BUSINESS IN PRACTICE

BMW is committed to producing a quality product. Every stage of the manufacturing process is inspected. Suppliers to BMW must also guarantee the quality of their components and materials.

Every employee of BMW is involved in checking quality. If problems are found, groups of employees from all levels of the hierarchy work together to solve the problems quickly.

 **TALK IT OVER**

Is this the main reason why BMW is successful?

The production of both goods and services involves costs which the business must pay.

COSTS

The **costs** of production in a business are divided into two main categories: *fixed costs* and *variable costs*.

Fixed costs are payments that must be made whether or not the business produces any goods. For example, a manufacturer must pay the interest on a loan even if there are no goods produced or sold, and a hairdresser must pay the rent for the shop even if there are no customers. Fixed costs are also known as **overheads** or **indirect costs**.

Variable costs change in direct proportion to output. For example, a manufacturer must pay for raw materials and packaging for every item produced, and a hairdresser must supply shampoo and hair products for every customer. Variable costs are also known as **direct costs**.

TALK IT OVER

What might the fixed and variable costs be in Greggs plc's bakery?

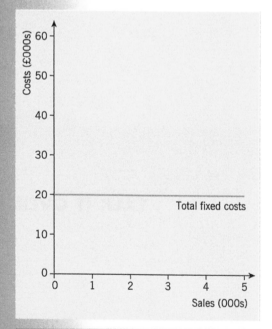

The total fixed costs are the same (£2000) whether 1000 items or 5000 items are sold

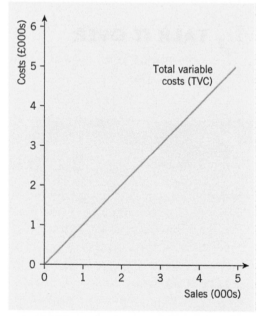

Each item has a variable cost of £1: 1000 items cost £1000; 5000 items cost £5000

REVENUE

Revenue is the *income* of a business. Usually this term means **sales revenue**, which is the income from selling goods or services.

Sales revenue is calculated from:

Sales revenue = quantity sold × price

 ## TALK IT OVER

What might the fixed and variable costs be in Greggs plc's shops?

BUSINESS IN PRACTICE

The business activity of Milfield Flying Club is to provide storage for customers' gliders and small aeroplanes, and to teach people to fly.

The gliders and small aeroplanes are stored in hangars. A caretaker looks after the maintenance of these hangars.

To provide flying lessons, the club needs aircraft and qualified instructors. Tuition is on a one-to-one basis. A full-time receptionist is employed to handle bookings and administration.

TALK IT OVER

What would be the fixed and variable costs of Milfield Flying Club? Why might wages be considered to be both fixed and variable costs?

It is important for a business to know when it will start to make a profit. It finds this out by calculating the amount of sales needed to cover costs.

BREAK-EVEN POINT

When a business **breaks even** it is making no profit and no loss – the total costs of production will be exactly the same as the income from sales. The **break-even point** is the point at which:

total costs (TC) = total revenue (TR)

Suppose Greggs plc were to produce 40 wedding cakes, and that the total cost of production for 40 wedding cakes was £4000. If 40 wedding cakes were sold for £100 each, the total revenue would be £4000. Greggs would make no profit, but nor would it make a loss – the business would break even. However, if 60 wedding cakes were sold for £100 each, Greggs would make £800 profit.

BREAK-EVEN CHARTS

A **break-even chart** can be constructed to find the break-even point.

Suppose that the price per cake is £100, the variable costs are £40 per cake, and the fixed costs are £2400.

Number of cakes sold	Total revenue: quantity × price (£)	Fixed costs (£)	Total variable cost: quantity × variable cost (£)	Total: fixed costs + variable cost (£)
0	0	2400	0	2400
20	2000	2400	800	3200
40	4000	2400	1600	4000
60	6000	2400	2400	4800

 TALK IT OVER

Can you think of a type of business which might have to 'break even' as one of its objectives?

If Greggs estimated sales at just 40 cakes, it would not risk production, because if just one cake *fewer* were sold, Greggs would make a loss.

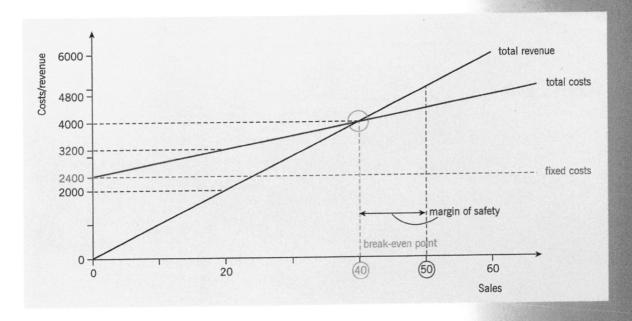

CALCULATING BREAK-EVEN

It is also possible to find the break-even point by **calculation**, using the **contribution** each sale makes to cover the fixed costs.

The amount of money from each sale after the variable costs have been covered is found from:

price – variable cost

Using the figures above:

£100–£40 = £60

This £60 can be used as a *contribution* towards covering the fixed costs. When the fixed costs are covered, the business will make a **profit**.

The fixed costs are £2400, so the number of cakes that need to be sold to cover the fixed costs is found from:

fixed costs/contribution = £2400/£60 = 40

40 cakes need to be sold to break even.

MARGIN OF SAFETY

The **margin of safety** is the range of output over which the business is able to make a profit. For example, if Greggs plc produces 50 wedding cakes, the margin of safety is 10 cakes – level of output (50) minus break-even point (40). It is useful for Greggs plc to know that sales could fall by 10 cakes before it made a loss.

 TALK IT OVER

What would be the break-even point if variable costs increased to £60 per cake?

KEY POINTS

■ **Break-even** – the point at which the costs are equal to the revenue.

■ **Break-even** charts and calculations can help to decide prices and predict profit.

TEST YOUR UNDERSTANDING

TOPICS 5–8

1 Why is stock control important?

2 Explain the difference between *minimum stock level* and *re-order level*.

3 Describe the factors that a business will consider when setting a maximum stock level.

4 What is *lead time*?

5 What is the difference between *quality control* and *quality assurance*?

6 Why might a customer be pleased to be given a warranty on a product?

7 Explain how the introduction of total quality management would affect the workforce of a business.

8 Use examples to explain the difference between *fixed costs* and *variable costs*.

9 Explain how a break-even chart can help decision-makers in a business.

10 Give another term which means the same as *sales revenue*.

CASE STUDY

Lazhar Mojaat owns and runs Picasso, a small restaurant that sells Italian food but that also offers specialities of Tunisian food. Some bigger premises have become vacant at a much better site in the same town. Lazhar wants to move his business to the new site and open a more up-market restaurant – Ristorante Verdi. Lazhar intends to keep Picasso open, but as a coffee shop.

The costs associated with opening Ristorante Verdi are:

– rent and rates: £8000

– heating, etc.: £2000

– furniture and decorating: £4000

– wages: £31 500.

The average cost of a meal is £4.

The average price of a meal in Picasso was £12. Lazhar does not think he could charge more than £18 in the new restaurant.

There was an average of 70 customers per week to Picasso. Lazhar expects a slight increase on this number – perhaps 80 customers per week.

1 What are the fixed costs for the new restaurant?

2 What are the variable costs for the new restaurant?

3 How many customers a year would Lazhar need to break even, if the average price charged was £18?

4 Could Lazhar afford to charge an average price *lower* than £18?

5 Explain how a break-even chart could help Lazhar make decisions if costs increase.

EXAM PRACTICE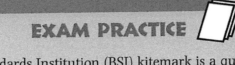

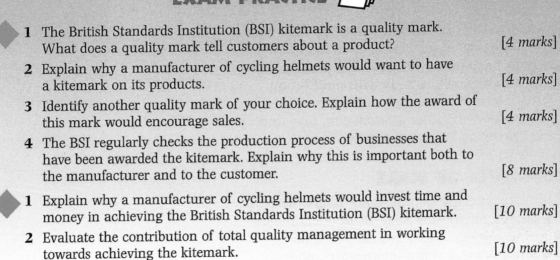

1 The British Standards Institution (BSI) kitemark is a quality mark. What does a quality mark tell customers about a product? *[4 marks]*

2 Explain why a manufacturer of cycling helmets would want to have a kitemark on its products. *[4 marks]*

3 Identify another quality mark of your choice. Explain how the award of this mark would encourage sales. *[4 marks]*

4 The BSI regularly checks the production process of businesses that have been awarded the kitemark. Explain why this is important both to the manufacturer and to the customer. *[8 marks]*

1 Explain why a manufacturer of cycling helmets would invest time and money in achieving the British Standards Institution (BSI) kitemark. *[10 marks]*

2 Evaluate the contribution of total quality management in working towards achieving the kitemark. *[10 marks]*

Not many businesses stay the same size; they have a tendency to grow bigger. There could be several reasons for increases in the size of a business, but the *main* reasons will be to do with profits, and trying to reduce business risks. A business might grow by diversifying, that is developing new and different products for new markets.

ECONOMIES OF SCALE

When a business grows, the **scale of production** increases. Increasing the scale of production can reduce the average cost of production. This reduction in costs is called **economies of scale**. When the average cost of producing each item is reduced, the business makes a bigger profit.

- The business will be able to order raw materials in **bulk**, and will receive **discounts** from suppliers. This makes the raw materials cheaper.
- **Advertising** will also become cheaper, as one advertisement can be used to promote several products instead of just one. This is especially true if a **brand name** is used.
- Growth often results in a wider **range of products**. This reduces the risk of financial difficulty if demand for one product falls.
- When the business grows, it is possible to use **division of labour** (see Unit 4, Topic 3). This can increase **efficiency**, not only on the production line but also in management, by using **specialists** such as accountants.
- An increase in output makes it worthwhile to buy **special machinery** and equipment which will be fully used.
- **Financial savings** can be made when borrowing from banks. Bigger businesses are considered to be 'safer' risks, and a **lower rate of interest** may be charged.

Too many layers of management

MARKET SHARE

As a business grows, its **market share** is likely to increase. This in turn improves the **security** of the business – the share value of a successful business will be quite high, which makes **takeovers** less likely. A large market share helps a business to deal with its competitors.

DISECONOMIES OF SCALE

Sometimes a business can grow *too* big, however, and costs can actually *rise*. This is due to **diseconomies of scale**. Too many layers of management may mean that managers lose contact with workers; the workers may then become demotivated because they feel that the management is not listening to them. Too much specialisation can slow down decision-making as so many people now need to be consulted.

Not all companies want to grow. Some want to stay small, because they feel the small business can offer a higher-quality individual product or service, and give personal attention – they like the direct contact with their customers. Some people like working on their own; and some want to stay in charge of their own business and not lose control to shareholders.

KEY POINTS

- **Economies of scale** – the more goods the company produces, the less it costs to produce one unit.

- Economies of scale can be:
  - **technical**: better equipment and specialisation improve efficiency
  - **marketing**: discounts for bulk buying
  - **administrative**: cutting costs in management
  - **financial**: borrowing money may be cheaper for big firms
  - **risk-bearing**: having a wide range of goods and markets spreads the risk.

BUSINESS IN PRACTICE

Richard Branson's Virgin Group is an example of economies of scale. The company uses risk-bearing economies. This means that the company's risks are spread: if one section of the business fails, the others are still there to carry on. If a drop in sales of a certain product should affect one part of the group's operations, other sections can keep the group going.

TALK IT OVER

Can you think of any other businesses that spread risks over a variety of activities? What disadvantages might this diversification cause?

Most businesses start off small, and grow in size by putting profits back into the business. This is called **internal growth**. This method of growth is often slow: if a business wants to grow more quickly it might consider a merger or a takeover. This is called **external growth**.

INTERNAL GROWTH

Internal growth is 'internal' because the business grows 'from the inside'. This method of growing is sometimes called **organic growth**.

Internal growth can be a result of an increase in demand for products. Demand may increase either because the products have become more popular in the home market, or because new demand is coming from more countries.

EXTERNAL GROWTH

External growth is 'external' because the business increases in size by adding an existing business, either through a merger or through a takeover. This method of growing is also referred to as **integration**, as one business becomes part of the other.

A **merger** is when two businesses *agree* to join together and become a single business. One company buys a majority of the other company's shares. Often the management of the company being taken over will advise the shareholders to sell their shares. This is a **friendly takeover**.

Some takeovers are not so friendly. For example, a business may want to remove competition, but the management of the competing business may not wish to merge. The first business may achieve the takeover by offering the shareholders of the competing business a very high price for their shares, thereby encouraging them to sell against their management's wishes. This is described as a **hostile takeover**.

BUSINESS IN PRACTICE

In 1965 Thomson Holidays (now the Thomson Travel Group) acquired Britannia Airways. Britannia Airways is now the world's largest holiday airline. A few years later, in 1972, Lunn Poly was bought by Thomson Holidays. Lunn Poly is now the biggest chain of travel agencies in the UK.

 TALK IT OVER

How might these mergers have benefited the consumer? Why might these mergers *not* be in the public interest?

INTEGRATION

There are different types of integration. **Vertical integration** describes integration of two businesses that produce the *same type of product*, but at *different stages* in the chain of production (see Unit 1, Topic 3). For example, Bird's Eye, which produces frozen foods, might buy out a number of vegetable producers. This kind of vertical integral integration would be known as **backward integration**, as the farmers are at an *earlier* stage in the chain of production than Bird's Eye. On the other hand, Greggs plc, which manufactures bread and cakes, acquired Bakers' Oven, a chain of bakery retailers. This was **forward integration**, because Bakers' Oven is at a *later* stage than Greggs in the chain of production.

Greggs' acquisition of Bakers' Oven is an example of forward integration

 TALK IT OVER

What advantages might Bird's Eye and Greggs have gained?

Horizontal integration describes a merger or takeover between businesses that produce the *same type of product*. For example, Dixon's, the electrical retailer, took over the Curry's chain with which it was in direct competition.

Conglomerate integration describes a merger or takeover between two businesses with very *different* products. This type of integration will increase profits and spread risks over a wider range of products. For example, Sainsbury plc took over the Texas do-it-yourself stores. This is also known as **diversification**.

External expansion is not always in the public's interest. This is especially true if the resulting business would have no competition – i.e. if it would have a **monopoly**. The **Competition Commission** (formerly the Monopolies and Mergers Commission) investigates such situations, and has the power to prevent the merger or takeover.

 **TALK IT OVER**

Is competition always good for consumers?

KEY POINTS

- **Merger** – two or more companies voluntarily joining together as equal partners.

- **Takeover** – one company taking control of another by buying shares, often at a price higher than the market value.

- Takeovers may be:
  - **friendly**: a large company takes over a smaller company to increase growth
  - **hostile**: a company takes over another company to remove a rival or to sell its assets and make a quick profit.

New technology

The introduction of **new technology** has significantly affected the business world.

MANUFACTURING GOODS

New technology has led to increases in productivity, which in turn reduce costs of production. Machines can be programmed to carry out operations continuously – they do not stop for lunch breaks or to go on holiday! Machines are consistently more accurate than humans, and operate much faster.

These improvements have been largely due to developments such as these:

◆ **Computer-aided design** (**CAD**) – products are designed more thoroughly, because the designer can change aspects of the design easily without having to start again.

◆ **Computer-aided manufacture** (**CAM**) – computers can control the production process, which is carried out by **computer numerical controlled** (**CNC**) machines.

◆ **CAD with CAM** – computers control the production process from design to manufacture.

◆ **Computer-integrated manufacturing** (**CIM**) – the whole production process can be linked, using a computer network: computer specialists oversee the manufacturing process, or part of the process, from a computer workstation.

This flexibility that new technology has introduced into manufacturing means that customers can have products made especially to their own specification – for example, a large business such as Levi can produce a pair of made-to-measure jeans.

PROVIDING SERVICES

CAD can be used to improve services such as kitchen design and landscape gardening. For example, a landscape gardener can *show* the client how the garden will look with plants and shrubs of different sizes and colours – and not only at different times of the year, but after one month, after one year, even after five years.

CAM

KEY POINTS

- **New technology** has had many effects on businesses:
  - increased productivity
  - better quality control
  - increase in demand for multiskilled workers
  - increase in unemployment for unskilled workers
  - new demands for workers to be more flexible and to have more training
  - new costs for acquiring or updating equipment.

- **CAM (computer-aided manufacture)** – computers used to control manufacturing processes.

- **CNC (computer numerically controlled)** – computers used to control machines cutting intricate shapes.

- **CAD (computer-aided design)** – computers used to design a product.

- **CIM (computer-integrated manufacturing)** – computers used to control extensive parts of the production process.

Retailing, too, is changing continually with the development of **e-commerce**. Estate agents can give prospective buyers 'virtual inspections' of properties, using their websites. Banking services are available over telephone lines and the Internet.

TALK IT OVER

Can you think of any goods or services that have improved over time, and the price of which has fallen?

EMPLOYMENT

Changes in technology have led to different skills being demanded by businesses. There is less demand for *unskilled* workers, and a greater demand for *multiskilled* employees.

BUSINESS IN PRACTICE

Telephone and Internet banking services are becoming more common. Bank customers can check balances, pay bills and make payments, all without having to leave home. Barclay's retail banking director commented that there has been a massive change in the way customers choose to bank. Barclay's closed 171 rural branches in 2000, and nearly 1000 more branches in recent years. In 1999 Barclay's made record profits of £2.4bn.

Extract from Derek Brown: 'Bank checks out to cash in', in *The Guardian*, 7.4.00

TALK IT OVER

Do you think customers benefit from the 'new technology'?

Some businesses are sited where they are because of tradition – for example, textiles in Lancashire – and others because that's where the owner *wants* the business to be! More usually, though, combinations of factors have influenced location decisions.

LAND AND PREMISES

Land and premises in towns and cities are much more highly priced than out-of-town green field sites. Green field sites are specially developed on rural land, and have a good supporting infrastructure.

There is more space on green field sites, and a chance to build a new factory rather than to adapt existing buildings. Out-of-town shopping areas take advantage of the availability of low-priced premises and a lot of space for customer parking.

TRANSPORT COSTS

Some businesses need to be near to raw materials and components, because the transport costs for bringing these goods would be very high. On the other hand, when finished goods are bulky and heavy, the business needs to be near to its customers.

All businesses need access to motorways or ports, and in some cases to both.

NEARNESS TO MARKET

Traditionally, service industries have needed to be near to their customers, but this is now changing for some. Clearly businesses such as hairdressers and restaurants do still need to be where they can easily be accessed by their customers. With the growth of direct selling and e-commerce, however, some retailers no longer need to be near to their market. Changes in methods of banking mean also that there is no need to have so many branches in towns and cities.

 TALK IT OVER

What type of businesses would need to be near raw materials?

 TALK IT OVER

What type of business would need to be near to its customers?

160

LABOUR

The availability of a **workforce** with appropriate **skills** is another important consideration. If there is no ready supply, the business will have to train workers, or to offer high wages to attract suitable people from other parts of the country. For example, Sunderland has seen an increase in call-centre businesses because there is a good supply of workers with the necessary skills.

GOVERNMENT

'**Footloose**' businesses do not need to consider transport costs or nearness to the market and so are free to locate anywhere in the country.

The government may give some kind of **aid** to attract footloose businesses to certain parts of the country:

◆ **Enterprise zones** are mainly inner-city areas. The government will offer aid by giving allowances for rents and rates.

◆ **Regional selective assistance** is available for certain areas, and **grants** are available to help businesses to buy machinery and provide training.

◆ **Urban development loans** are available to businesses whose presence will help to regenerate urban areas.

◆ **European Union** (EU) **grants** are available to areas which meet certain conditions, such as high levels of unemployment.

KEY POINTS

■ **Business location** depends on:
– availability of land and premises
– cost of transport
– nearness to market
– availability of labour
– government aid.

■ **Footloose** – businesses that can be located anywhere.

■ **Infrastructure** – transport systems and support services such as hospitals and schools.

 TALK IT OVER

Why might the government want to attract businesses to certain areas?

BUSINESS IN PRACTICE

Seventy per cent of Japanese computer games are designed within a 30-mile radius of Liverpool. Firms include Psygnosis, currently updating the 'Formula One' game for Playstation 2, and Rage Software, one of Europe's largest game developers. One employer commented, 'We are in the e-business, location isn't necessarily an issue.' He said his company relied on the local universities for staff.

In Liverpool a three-bedroom semi costs between £60 000 and £130 000, and Manchester international airport is a half-hour drive away. Liverpool received almost

£1bn from the European Development Fund, and the growth of hi-tech business has helped to reduce unemployment from almost 20% in 1990 to 9.5% today.

Extract from Anne Hyland: 'Mersey beats faster to the hi-tech sound', *The Guardian*, 6.6.00

 TALK IT OVER

If location is not an issue for e-business, why might the North West Development Agency receive approximately 300 enquiries a year from the hi-tech firms that want to locate in Liverpool?

TEST YOUR UNDERSTANDING

TOPICS 9–12

1 What are *economies of scale*?
2 Explain why a business might want to grow, *other* than to achieve economies of scale.
3 Explain how a business can grow too big.
4 What is the difference between *internal* and *external* growth?
5 Give an example of each of the different types of integration.
6 How can a public limited company be taken over even if its owners do not want it to be?
7 What is the difference between CAD, CAM and CIM?
8 List the advantages of using CAD.
9 Explain why computers have led to increased productivity in manufacturing.
10 Explain what is meant by a *footloose business*.

CASE STUDY

For nearly 40 years Nestlé has had a factory based at Dalston in Cumbria. The production of Nescafé Cappuccino moved to Dalston in 1992 because the factory had a reputation for teamwork and flexibility.

The land at Dalston was suitable, being in the heart of a prime dairy area and near to water for processing. The cost of transporting the milk, which is the main raw material, is minimised because fresh milk can be collected daily from suppliers.

Dalston is near to a road system that links it with major ports. This is important, as all milk powder products are exported.

Although Dalston is a small village in a rural region, it is easy to find multiskilled labour.

1 Describe the factors that affect the location of a business.
2 Explain why Nestlé moved the production of Nescafé Cappuccino to Dalston.
3 Why was the road system important to Nestlé?
4 Why might the pool of available labour be multiskilled?
5 Do you think Nestlé made the right choice in moving Nescafé Cappuccino to Dalston? Give reasons for your answer.

EXAM PRACTICE

1 Explain the difference between a *merger* and *takeover*. [4 marks]
2 What are the advantages of *vertical mergers*? [4 marks]
3 How could shareholders be persuaded to hold their shares? [2 marks]
4 Are mergers always in the public interest? [8 marks]

1 Explain why a business might want to acquire an existing business. [10 marks]
2 Evaluate the impact of mergers on the stakeholders of a business. [10 marks]

UNIT 5 Finance

TOPIC 1   Functions of business finance

Every business needs **finance**:

◆ to start up the business
◆ for the day-to-day running of the business
◆ for business growth.

FINANCIAL PLANNING

Good **financial planning** is at the heart of any successful business – without it the business will fail. Financial decisions have to be made in every section of the business. For example:

◆ The human resources department has to make financial decisions on the cost of paying **wages**: how many staff does the business need, and how much can it afford to pay them?

◆ The **marketing** budget influences the type of marketing campaign the business can afford.

◆ In the **production** department, the amount of available finance will dictate whether the business can invest in new technology, expand, or relocate to a new site.

All of these are major financial decisions which need to be taken by the managers and owners of the business, and which need a great deal of planning.

TALK IT OVER

To which departments would a finance manager have to speak in order to carry out his or her job?

164

MAIN AREAS OF FINANCE

There are five main areas of finance that any business has to deal with. They are:

◆ **Cash-flow forecasting** – planning the cash flowing in and out of the business to make sure that there is always enough money in the business to pay the bills.

◆ **Budget planning** – setting the financial budgets for the business and for the individual departments.

◆ **Raising finance** – analysing financial needs, and selecting the most appropriate sources of finance for a particular project.

◆ **Management accounting** – identifying methods of controlling costs to make the business more efficient and thus increase profits. Management accounting also provides managers with information on performance and efficiency, which helps them make decisions about the running of the business.

◆ **Financial accounting** – drawing up and interpreting the financial records of the business, and producing an analysis and evaluation of its finances for internal or external use.

KEY POINTS

The five main areas of finance are:

■ cash-flow forecasting
■ budget planning
■ raising finance
■ management accounting
■ financial accounting.

BUSINESS IN PRACTICE

Sam Theodorou is the Chief Accountant for Humberside Tools, a public limited company that has three main divisions: International, Industrial, and Commercial. The business manufactures saws and other cutting tools, for a variety of customers from DIY enthusiasts to large construction companies.

Sam's day begins with a 7.30 breakfast meeting. He is meeting with the manager of the Commercial Division to discuss her budget. Sam is concerned that a number of setbacks in the R&D plans for a new product have caused the division to overspend. It is Sam's job to get to the bottom of the problem and put the division back on track.

The remainder of the morning is spent pricing an order from a Korean company.

Sam has to calculate the cost of the job and to decide on a price to charge. He also has to make sure the International Division has enough cash to purchase the raw materials and parts for the order.

After a lunch meeting with his line manager to discuss this month's sales figures, Sam spends his afternoon with his team of accountants preparing some of the accounts for the Annual Report. It is due to be published in less than a month, and there is still a lot to be done.

 TALK IT OVER

Identify the main areas of finance on which Sam Theodorou worked during this working day.

WHY DO BUSINESSES NEED FINANCIAL FORECASTING?

Financial forecasting has a wide range of uses. It is used by the business:

- to help in decision-making
- to assess the profitability of the business
- to plan strategies
- to control resources
- to measure the efficiency of the business
- to forecast possible future trends.

Before a business can plan how it is going to use its finances, it needs to try to forecast what is likely to happen in the future, and what will be needed by the business. To work this out, the finance department will collect information on what has happened in the past, and use this to help predict what is likely to happen in the future.

Cash-flow forecasting predicts the receipts into and payments from a business

 TALK IT OVER

How could a business predict next year's sales figures? What factors might affect the accuracy of this prediction?

CASH-FLOW FORECASTING

Cash-flow forecasting is a very important part of a business's financial forecasting. It is a prediction of the cash that will flow *into* the business (the **receipts**), and the cash that will flow *out of* the business (the **payments**). From the cash-flow forecast, the managers will hope to foresee any possible cash-flow problems and take action to avoid them. For example, there is not enough cash in June so the business can either delay paying creditors or arrange for an overdraft.

A business's cash-flow forecast is often looked at by lenders to make sure that it would not be too risky to invest in the business.

	April	May	June
Receipts (cash inflow)	3,300	3,300	2,600
MINUS			
Payments (cash outflow)	3,300	3,200	3,000
Net cash flow (for month)	0	100	(-400)
PLUS			
Opening balance (at start of month)	2,000	2,000	3,000
=			
Closing balance (at end of month)	2,000	2,100	2,600

CASH-FLOW STATEMENT

A **cash-flow statement** is a record of all incomes and expenditures that actually happened in a given time period.

CASH-FLOW PROBLEMS

If a business does not have sufficient cash to cover day-to-day expenditure, it is said to have a **cash-flow problem**.

A cash-flow problem may be due to customers taking goods on **credit**. This means that sales and profits have been made, but the cash has not yet been received. Another reason might be that the business has used a lot of its cash to buy stocks, but has not yet been able to sell these. Until the business sells this stock, it will not receive any cash.

DEALING WITH A CASH-FLOW PROBLEM

If a business forecasts a cash-flow problem, it can arrange an **overdraft** or try to buy more of its raw materials using **trade credit**. It could also try to make sure that most of its customers pay for their purchases straight away.

KEY POINTS

■ **Financial forecasting** is necessary in order to predict what is likely to happen in the future.

BUSINESS IN PRACTICE

Even successful businesses can fail if they find themselves having cash-flow problems.

Whitecliffe Upholsteries was a well-established business that had been operating for over six years. It had a good reputation and a healthy market share in the North West of England.

In 1997 the business's owner made the decision to offer customers sales on credit. The business was under pressure to do this because so many larger furniture stores were offering customers very attractive credit deals.

The decision to offer credit was a huge success – and a huge failure. Many customers took up the 'Buy now, pay later' offer. Sofas and armchairs sold quickly. Unfortunately,

however, Whitecliffe did not receive money for the furniture immediately – in fact customers did not have to pay anything for six months, and then they were required to pay only an instalment. Whitecliffe found itself with insufficient funds to buy more stock – or even pay its bills. The bank was not sympathetic, and Whitecliffe had no option but to close down – six months after it had initially offered customers credit. Whitecliffe Upholsteries no longer exists.

 TALK IT OVER

How could Whitecliffe have avoided its cash-flow problem?

TEST YOUR UNDERSTANDING

TOPICS 1–2

1 Give three functions of the finance department.
2 Give three reasons why businesses need finance.
3 What is the purpose of a cash-flow forecast?
4 Why would a lender want to see a cash-flow forecast?
5 Explain the difference between a *cash receipt* and a *cash payment*.
6 How could you calculate *net cash flow*?
7 List six reasons why businesses need to forecast finance.
8 What is the difference between a cash-flow forecast and a cash-flow statement?
9 What is the difference between *management accounting* and *financial accounting*?
10 How might a business deal with a cash-flow problem?

CASE STUDY

Picture House Ltd is a medium-sized cinema in the centre of a small town. It has recently extended its premises, and now houses three screens. It manages to show the latest releases to a local market – mainly teenagers and young families – with two evening screenings and weekend matinees.

The forecasted receipts and payments have been calculated by a local accountant. The expected receipts in the next 6 months are:

£(000)	July	Aug.	Sept.	Oct.	Nov.	Dec.
	84	68	80	88	96	120

These figures include ticket sales, and refreshments sold at the confectionery booth inside the cinema.

Picture House Ltd does however have payments to make. The accountant predicts:

£(000)	July	Aug.	Sept.	Oct.	Nov.	Dec.
Purchase of confectionery stock	14	11	13	15	16	20
New release films	6	6	6	6	8	8
Staff wages	11	11	11	11	12	13
Utilities	2	2	2	2	3	3
Advertising	15	15	15	30	30	25
Loan repayments	20	20	20	20	20	20
Miscellaneous	3	3	4	3	5	4

The closing balance of cash in June is (£17).

1 Using the information you have been given, produce a cash-flow forecast for Picture House Ltd.

2 Explain why sales receipts are higher in the winter months.

3 In which months does Picture House Ltd have a cash shortage?

4 Suggest two ways in which Picture House Ltd could solve its cash-flow problems in these months.

5 Give three reasons why figures on this forecast may be incorrect.

6 Give two advantages of using computer software to generate this cash-flow forecast.

Limited companies, both private and public, are obliged by law to produce an audited **balance sheet** each year. The balance sheet is a record of the assets and liabilities of the company. It is an indicator of the *value* of the business. (For more about balance sheets, see Unit 5, Topic 11.)

Every business has assets and liabilities.

ASSETS

Assets are what the business owns. Assets may include buildings, plant and equipment, stock, and cash in the bank. Assets may also include money owed to the business by other businesses. Assets are classed as *fixed* and *current*.

Fixed assets include buildings, machinery and equipment, computers and vehicles. Fixed assets are items that are likely to stay in the business for a reasonable length of time – more than a year. Assets that can be seen and touched are called **tangible assets**. Other assets, such as investments or goodwill, are known as **intangible assets**.

Goodwill is the *loyalty* customers have to a particular company. If they are happy with the product or service they receive, they will return again and again. Goodwill is difficult to calculate, but it has a significant value to the business.

Current assets include stock, debtors (people who owe money to the business), and cash. These may all change in value from day to day. Current assets can also be easily changed into money, and are called **liquid assets**.

There are three main categories of current assets: *stock*, *debtors* and *cash*. **Stock** comprises:

- **raw materials** bought to make the goods
- **work in progress** – goods while they are being made
- **finished goods** ready for sale.

Debtors are:

- outside businesses and people who owe the business money for goods that they have bought –

BUSINESS IN PRACTICE

Sir Tom Farmer is the founder of Kwik-Fit Holdings, and was its largest individual shareholder until its takeover by Ford.

Sir Tom had made his first fortune by the age of 28, building up a tyre business which he sold to an American company.

In 1971 he set up Kwik-Fit with some friends. The business has been extremely successful since then, and has grown into one of the world's largest automative parts, repairs and replacement specialists.

The company has also expanded abroad, buying up the French company Speedy and the German company Pitstop. This deal added 568 outlets to its existing 1291 branches in the UK, Ireland, Belgium and the Netherlands.

It has also diversified into new markets, offering motor insurance policies and a national breakdown service, Kwik-Fit Auto Save Club.

Adapted from *Business Review*, 11.99

 TALK IT OVER

What might be the assets and liabilities of a company such as Kwik-Fit Holdings?

most businesses allow other businesses to buy from them on credit, giving a period of time for payment after delivery.

Cash is:

◆ money in the bank
◆ petty cash within the business
◆ other cash that the business has in hand.

LIABILITIES

Liabilities are what the business owes to others. **Current liabilities** are the amounts of money that will have to be paid back within the next 12 months.

The most common current liabilities are:

◆ **trade creditors** – outside businesses to which the business owes money for goods bought
◆ bank **overdrafts**
◆ **dividends** for shareholders.

Long-term liabilities are amounts of money that will have to be paid back in *more* than 12 months' time. The most common long-term liabilities are:

◆ long-term **loans** and **debentures**
◆ **mortgages**
◆ **taxes** owed.

WORKING CAPITAL

Every business needs **working capital**. This is the money the business has readily available – or expects to have soon – which enables it to pay for day-to-day costs such as paying wages or buying raw materials. The working capital is also called the **net current assets**.

Working capital is calculated as follows:

working capital = current assets – current liabilities

If the business is running efficiently, it will normally have current *assets* of between one and two times the value of its current *liabilities*. With this level of coverage the business should have enough capital to deal with most unforeseen problems. If the business increases output, it must also increase working capital; otherwise it may have cash-flow problems later on, which could threaten the future of the business.

KEY POINTS

■ **Assets** – what the business owns, such as:
  – buildings
  – plants
  – equipment
  – stock
  – money in the bank
  – debts owed by others to the business.

■ Assets can be:
  – **fixed**: assets that are likely to retain the same value
  – **current**: assets that change value often
  – **tangible**: assets that can be touched and seen
  – **intangible**: assets that have no physical form
  – **liquid**: assets that can easily be turned into money.

■ **Liabilities** – what the business owes.

■ Liabilities can be:
  – **current**: debts that must be paid within 12 months
  – **long term**: debts paid back over more than 12 months.

■ **Working capital** or **net current assets** – the value of current assets minus current liabilities.

■ Working capital is used to pay for day-to-day costs.

All businesses need **finance** to be able to operate. This finance can be classified into three main areas.

- to **start up** the business,
- for the **day-to-day running** of the business
- for business **growth**.

START-UP CAPITAL

Start-up capital is the money that is needed to set up the business and to buy fixed assets such as land, buildings, vehicles, plant and equipment. Such purchases form the business's **capital expenditure**.

REVENUE EXPENDITURE

The money that is needed to cover the costs of the day-to-day running of the business is called **revenue expenditure**. This is the money needed for such things as mortgage, rates and wages. Revenue expenditure is funded by **working capital** (see Unit 5, Topic 11).

GROWTH

Once a business has been established and starts to make a profit, the owners will often want to expand. Finance will be needed for items such as more stock, wages, and advertising.

TALK IT OVER

Identify a range of different types of businesses and compare the different amounts of start-up capital they might need.

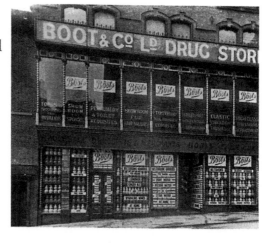

Boots is an example of a business that has expanded since it was established

CAPITAL EXPENDITURE

Capital expenditure can be financed by using either **internal sources** of finance such as profits, or **external sources** such as bank loans. Some items of capital expenditure, such as land and buildings, will need **long-term borrowing** to finance them. Internal sources of finance would not be sufficient on their own, so the business will need to look at external sources such as a bank loan.

The advantages of using an *internal* source of finance are that the money does not have to be repaid, there are no interest charges to be added on and the structure of the business remains the same.

KEY POINTS

- **Revenue expenditure** – money used for the day-to-day running of the business, paid for by working capital.

- **Capital expenditure** – money used to start the business and to make large purchases such as new machinery.

- Finance is raised either internally or externally.

BUSINESS IN PRACTICE

Whistler's is a small chain of fast-food outlets based in New Zealand. Its aim is to provide a variety of good-quality foods for families on an average income.

Whistler's aims to attract customers similar to those who use McDonald's, Burger King or Pizza Hut.

The restaurants are usually situated in out-of-town shopping areas. They have large car parks and benches, and umbrellas for picnics.

Inside the standard Whistler's restaurant are segmented dining areas around a central salad bar. The seating is comfortable and there are plenty of facilities for young children.

Adapted from J. Rowley: *Business Studies Magazine*, 10.95

 TALK IT OVER

Identify (a) the start-up costs and (b) the day-to-day running costs for one Whistler outlet.

Whistler's is currently a small chain of restaurants. One way it could grow would be to increase sales. (a) State two further ways in which the Whistler chain could grow. (b) What expenditure would be needed for each of these courses of action?

The sources of capital available to different types of businesses varies greatly. For the sole trader, the sources are limited to:

- any money the owner has in the **bank** – for example, redundancy money or savings
- **personal assets** such as a car or house, which the owner may sell to help finance the business
- the **profits** from the business, which can be reinvested into the business
- **retained profits** from the business – previously invested in a bank **deposit** account for any emergencies that might arise.

Larger companies have access to more sources of finance, including issuing more shares.

I was hoping to get £500 more than than you're offering. I know it is worth it.

Personal assets can be a source of finance

SHARES

Limited companies can raise capital by selling *more shares*. The only problem with this is that the shareholders may want a bigger say in the running of the business.

The company can '**go public**'. A private limited company may decide to become a public limited company, and invite the general public to buy shares in the company. The company needs the approval of the Stock Exchange Council before it can be **floated** on the Stock Exchange (see Unit 1, Topic 9).

Alternatively a **rights issue** of new shares is the most common internal source of finance used by *public limited companies*. The rights issue gives current shareholders the right to buy more shares, in proportion to the number they own already. In this way the *balance of control* in the business is not changed. For example, Eurotunnel went back to its shareholders on several occasions to try to raise more capital as the cost of building the Channel Tunnel went up.

 TALK IT OVER

What would be the advantages and disadvantages to a private limited company of 'going public'?

Two main types of shares are available. **Ordinary shares** are the largest single form of long-term capital used by businesses. The ordinary shareholder may receive a share of the profits in the form of a **dividend**. The dividend may vary, according to the amount of profit made by the business, and the amount kept back by the directors for **reinvestment** in the company, which is called **retained profits**.

Preference shares also give the shareholder part-ownership in the company. However, the preference shareholder is paid a *fixed* dividend, and has priority over the ordinary shareholder when the profits are shared out. In a good year, therefore, the return in dividends to a preference shareholder may be less than that to an ordinary shareholder, as the risk taken is smaller.

Venture capitalists are risk-takers who invest in companies (usually small companies), and make a return on their investment. They help to build up the company; in return, they may want a seat on the Board of Directors, shares in the company, or interest on their investment.

ASSETS

Selling assets is another way of raising capital. For example, a sole trader might sell off a large van and buy a smaller one. Similarly, a medium-sized company might sell off factory space or land that it was not using; and large businesses might sell subsidiary businesses to raise money.

SALE AND LEASEBACK

Sale and leaseback is a further internal source of finance. In this case, the business sells one of its main buildings to a financial institution – such as a pension fund company – and then leases it back from them. The business now has to pay rent to the financial institution, but has raised a large amount of capital from the sale of the property. This source of finance is commonly used by public limited companies, but may also be used by private limited companies and sole traders.

 TALK IT OVER

Which of the sources of capital described in this topic would be unsuitable for a new business?

KEY POINTS

- Internal source of finance
  - finance from within the business
  - selling assets
  - reinvesting profits
  - sale and leaseback.

- External source of finance
  - finance from outside the business
  - owners' capital, e.g. sole trader's savings,
  - share issue
  - venture capital.

- **Rights issue** – offering more shares to existing shareholders.

- **Ordinary shares** or **equities** – the shareholder receives a share of the profits (a **dividend**) and has part-ownership of the business.

- **Preference shares** – the shareholder receives a fixed sum and has part ownership of the company.

To raise the finance it needs, a business will sometimes need to look to **external sources** of borrowing.

SMALLER BUSINESSES

For small businesses, the external sources are few. A loan from **relatives** and **friends** is one option. The problem with this is that they might then want a say in the running of the business.

The government sponsors a number of schemes to help small businesses set up:

◆ **Loans** may be available in specific areas identified by the government as needing assistance – for example, some inner-city areas.

◆ The **Small Firms Loan Guarantee Scheme**, available from the banks, has government-backed guarantees to support small-business owners who do not have enough money to obtain conventional loans for their business. It applies to new and existing small businesses in the manufacturing, construction and service industries. The banks offer **start-up loans** for small businesses – the owners choose the length of time to be taken in paying back the loan, and whether to take out the loan with a fixed or variable rate of interest. The bank will need some **security** as guarantee for the loan, such as the owner's house.

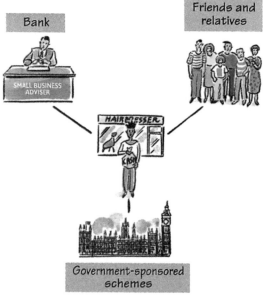

Bank

Friends and relatives

SMALL BUSINESS ADVISER

HAIRDRESSER

Government-sponsored schemes

Sources of finance for small businesses

DEBENTURES

Debentures are long-term loans issued by limited companies. They have a fixed rate of interest and an agreed **repayment** date. Unlike a share, a debenture is not permanent, and the debenture holder receives interest in payment for the loan. The debenture holder is not a part-owner of the business.

Larger businesses find it easier to borrow money from financial institutions

Newshires Bank

STARTING A BUSINESS

Borrowing ▪ **Insurance** ▪ **Information**

▪

BORROWING

Overdraft
This is short-term borrowing, available to cover cash-flow problems. It is paid back within a number of months.

Loan
This is medium-term borrowing, available for the purchase of such things as equipment. It is paid back over a few years.

Mortgage
This is long-term borrowing, available for the purchase of business premises and other large assets. It is paid back over a number of years – between 10 and 50.

INSURANCE

You are required to take out insurance when you agree to any borrowing.

Newshires Bank provides an excellent policy through our partner, Newshires Insurance Company (see leaflet INSX2).

You may, of course, go elsewhere for your insurance. However, it is essential that you provide us with proof that you are covered.

KEY POINTS

▪ Sources of long term borrowing include:
- debentures
- mortgage
- government loans
- hire purchase.

▪ Limited companies can raise finance through debentures.

MORTGAGE

A business of any size could obtain a **mortgage**. A mortgage is a loan that is secured on property. If the borrower does not keep up the repayments, the property could be **repossessed** by the lender.

LOANS OR GRANTS

The European Union, central government and local government all have schemes that provide **loans** or **grants** to help businesses.

 TALK IT OVER

Even though loans mean that the borrower has to pay interest, many owners prefer to borrow than provide their own finance. Why might this be?

When capital expenditure is needed, for vehicles, computers, plant and equipment, several methods can be used by any business. These sources are not long-term.

HIRE PURCHASE

This source of finance is useful for capital expenditure (fixed assets), e.g. vehicles. Hire purchase means that the goods are the property of the hire-purchase company until the last payment has been made. A **deposit** has to be paid, and regular **instalments** paid (usually monthly). The payments include a rate of interest for use of the hire-purchase scheme. The borrower does not own the asset until the last instalment has been paid.

LEASING

Leasing is paid by fixed instalments over a period of time, usually one to three years. During the lease period the sole trader never owns the items, but at the end of the lease there is an **option to** buy. Leasing is most useful for items such as computers and cars for which models are regularly upgraded: leasing allows the business to keep up with the latest technology.

CONTRACT HIRE

Contract hire is paid by **rental** for a fixed period of time. Contract hire is often used for vehicles or plant and equipment, and a **maintenance contract** can be taken out with the hire. The items remain the property of the business that supplied them for hire.

OVERDRAFT

Businesses may also need short-term loans to cover day-to-day running costs – **revenue expenditure** For revenue expenditure a business needs to use short-term borrowing. Frequently an **overdraft** is used as a short-term solution to cash-flow problems, such as a need for short-term cash, to handle a time delay between purchasing goods and receiving payment for them, or unexpected but limited expenditure items. Overdrafts are flexible, but interest is charged on a daily basis.

Banks can help by providing mortgages and overdrafts

 TALK IT OVER
What advice would you give a small business looking for a way to finance the purchase of a photocopier?

TRADE CREDIT

When the business buys goods or services on credit, it is not always necessary to pay for them immediately. Payment is delayed for a set period of time, usually a month. No interest is paid during this time, but the business may lose the chance of cash discounts if the payment is not made on time.

DEBT FACTORING

If the business is owed money from customers who have bought goods but not yet paid for them, the business can ask a **debt factoring** business to give it the sum it is owed. In return for a fee, the factoring business collects the debts owed. Debt factoring saves the business from chasing the debts itself, but it has to pay a price for the service provided.

 TALK IT OVER

Why might some smaller businesses consider debt factoring to be a very useful service?

 KEY POINTS

- Limited companies can raise finance through **debentures**.
- **Capital expenditure** is money spent on fixed assets.
- **Revenue expenditure** can be financed by:
  - overdrafts
  - trade credit
  - debt factoring.
  These are all forms of **short-term borrowing**.

BUSINESS IN PRACTICE

Reverberation is a musical producer based in North Wales. The business consists of two technicians and the producer-owner, Oliver Jackson. Oliver and his staff work from converted farm buildings which house two recording studios.

Artists have travelled from all over Europe to record tracks with the Reverberation team. The team specialises in club anthems and mixes that make full use of the latest music technology.

Oliver began the business two years ago with £10 000 he inherited from his father. The business has not grown in size over the last two years, although its name is becoming more widely recognised, especially in some of the clubbers' holiday resorts. In its third year a small profit has been forecast, but Oliver is cautious and maintains that he will always try to spread his expenditure as much as possible.

 TALK IT OVER

Discuss three ways in which Oliver could spread his expenditure and avoid any large payments.

What risks does Oliver face regarding the future of his business?

If a business needs to raise finance, there are a number of issues it needs to take into account:

- the cost to the business of raising the finance
- what the business intends to use the funds for – is it short-term or long-term?
- the current trading position of the business
- the balance between the need for the capital and the desire not to get in debt.

COSTS

When a business wants to borrow money, there are several **costs** involved:

- the interest rate to be paid back if a loan is taken out
- the legal costs and fees paid to the broker if shares are being issued
- the extra dividends paid out to new shareholders
- the administrative fees charged by factoring companies
- the seat on the Board or shares acquired by the venture capitalist
- the charges paid to hire-purchase, leasing and contract-hire companies.

When deciding on the best way to raise finance, all of these costs have to be balanced against each other. If interest rates are *low* the alternatives to loans become less attractive, as they have extra costs such as administrative costs or legal fees. If interest rates are *high* the alternatives become much more attractive.

USE OF FUNDS

If the capital is needed for a *long-term* investment (such as the purchase of land or building), the business will need to consider long-term methods of raising finance, such as mortgage loans, venture capital or share issues.

If the capital is needed for *medium-term* investment (such as vehicles, plant and equipment), medium-term methods of raising finance, such as debentures, retained profits, hire purchase and leasing, should all

The purchase of land and buildings requires long-term investment

---

Credit is only available to those aged over 18 and whose application is suitable.

Mortgage loans are available from The Bank, High St, NEWTOWN, NW2 2HP.

For a written quotation please write to Customer Services, The Bank, High St, NEWTOWN, NW2 2HP, or ask at one of our branches.

You are obliged to provide security and arrange insurance for mortgage loans.

YOUR HOME IS AT RISK IF YOU DO NOT KEEP UP THE REPAYMENTS ON A MORTGAGE OR OTHER LOAN SECURED ON IT.

Long-term investment

Cash price £1000 including VAT & delivery. Pay nil deposit and nothing for 12 months. After 12 months pay the total amount (£1000) interest free. APR 0% only if loan is repaid after 12 months. Finance also available over a longer period of 3 years at APR 26.6%. No deposit, no payments for 12 months then 24 payments of £65.79. Total price £1579.00.

Medium-term investment

be considered: each offers different facilities to the business. For example, with retained profits there are no repayments.

If the capital is needed for *short-term* finance (such as cash-flow problems, or buying raw materials), short-term methods of raising finance, such as trade credit or overdraft facilities, should be considered: these offer low interest rates or no interest to be paid at all.

THE TRADING POSITION OF THE BUSINESS

The **timing** of raising finance is important. Limited companies have to produce annual accounts, so financial institutions will be aware of the financial state of the business.

If the business is showing good profits, it will find it much easier to borrow money. If the business is looking less profitable, it may have to look to people like venture capitalists to raise finance, as they are more willing to take a risk.

THE BALANCE BETWEEN DEBT AND CAPITAL

The balance between *debt* and *capital* is called **gearing**. It is the balance between the amount of money a business has raised through long-term loans (debts) and the amount of money it has raised from the owners (capital).

The business must make sure that the ratio of debt to capital is not too high. Too much debt makes the business a risky investment.

 TALK IT OVER

If you were giving advice to a business that needed finance, what questions would you ask before giving your advice?

The purchase of vehicles, plant and equipment requires medium-term investment

KEY POINTS

Factors that influence the source of finance include:

- the costs of raising the finance
- the duration of any finance deals
- what the finance will be used for
- the current trading position of the company
- the balance between debt and capital.

All businesses, large and small, need to keep accurate records of every financial transaction in the business. For example, whenever a sale or purchase is made, a record must be kept.

These records are called the **accounts**. Large businesses will employ an accountant, but sole traders have to record their financial transactions themselves, or pay an accountant to keep the records.

All businesses need to know what is happening to their money on a day-by-day basis. They must be able to answer questions such as:

◆ How is the business performing?

◆ Can the debts be paid?

◆ What taxes need to be paid?

◆ Can the business afford to expand?

Large businesses will employ accountants

ACCOUNTING

Accounting means the methods and procedures used to keep a record of financial activities within the business. This information is then used by stakeholders to see how well the business is doing.

◆ **Managers** want to see the accounts to help them make decisions and plan the future of the business.

◆ **Shareholders** want to see the accounts to find out whether the value of their shares has increased.

◆ **Potential shareholders** want to see the accounts to decide whether it is worth investing in the business.

◆ **Employees** want to see the accounts to find out how the business is performing and to check that their jobs are secure.

 TALK IT OVER

Why must records be kept of a business's purchases?

In millions of CHF (except for per share data)		January/June 2000	January/June 1999	
Sales		38 784	35 277	
EBITDA [a]		5 867	5 010	[a] Earnings Before Interest, Taxes, Depreciation and Amortisation.
as % of sales		15.1%	14.2%	
EBITA [b]		4 500	3 681	[b] Earnings Before Interest, Taxes and Amortisation.
as % of sales		11.6%	10.4%	
Trading profit		4 296	3 461	
as % of sales		11.1%	9.8%	
Net profit		2 798	2 079	
as % of sales		7.2%	5.9%	
Expenditure on tangible fixed assets		1 327	1 171	
Equity, end June		26 386	22 208	
Market capitalisation, end June		126 085	108 289	
Per share:				
Net profit	CHF	72.7	53.5	
Equity, end June	CHF	686	571	

Principal key figures in USD [c]		January/June 2000	January/June 1999	[c] Figures translated at end June rates.
In millions of USD (except for per share data)				
Sales		23 794	22 759	
EBITDA [a]		3 599	3 232	
EBITA [b]		2 761	2 375	
Trading profit		2 636	2 233	
Net profit		1 717	1 341	
Equity, end June		16 188	14 328	
Market capitalisation, end June		77 353	69 864	
Per share:				
Net profit	USD	44.6	34.5	
Equity, end June	USD	421	368	

◆ **Creditors** want to see the accounts to check whether it is safe to give the business credit in the future.

◆ The **Inland Revenue** wants to see the accounts to make an accurate assessment of the taxes due.

There are rules about how financial transactions must be recorded, and the sort of information that is put in different accounts. Most of this information has to be made public. For example, limited companies must publish a **trading account**, a **profit and loss account**, and a **balance sheet**. These are all published in the company's audited **annual report and accounts**. The annual accounts, also called the **final accounts**, are a financial statement summary drawn up at the end of the year's trading.

 TALK IT OVER

If a business's annual accounts show a very successful year, how might the different stakeholders react?

Business people need to keep accurate accounts which the Inland Revenue can check

KEY POINTS

■ **Accounting** – the way financial activity is recorded and used.

■ The business's **performance**, as shown in the accounts, is used by stakeholders such as:
 – managers
 – owners
 – employees
 – creditors
 – the Inland Revenue.

■ Registered companies must produce an audited **financial report** and make it public.

■ An **annual report** has:
 – a **trading, profit and loss account**
 – a **balance sheet**
 – statements on the position of the business.

 TALK IT OVER

Why must limited companies make their financial information available to the public?

The **trading account** is the simplest of the accounts, and is a record of the **gross profit** of the business.

To work out the gross profit, the accountant has to know the amount of money coming in from selling goods or services, and how much it actually costs to produce or buy these goods or services.

Picture House Ltd is a small group of cinemas located on the outskirts of London. Opposite is the trading account for refreshments sold by Picture House Ltd.

The trading account does not take any overheads (indirect costs) into consideration – it is purely the profit from buying and selling (trading).

gross profit = sales revenue – cost of sales

However, a business will not sell all its stock by the end of the year. There will always be some stock from the previous financial year waiting to be sold – the closing stock – which becomes the opening stock for the next financial year.

KEY POINTS

- **Gross profit** – profit before overheads and expenses are deducted.

- **Trading account** – a simple record of gross profit.

- **Cost of sales** – the value of the stock that has been sold during the year.

End of financial year

Sales during the year

Closing stock

Beginning of next financial year

Sales during the year

The trading account will make an adjustment for changes in stock levels and calculate the cost of sales for that particular financial year:

opening stock + purchases (minus any returns) – closing stock = cost of sales

BUSINESS IN PRACTICE

Picture House Ltd
Trading Account for year ended 31 December 20X1

	£	£
Sales Revenue *A*		200 000
Opening Stock (refreshments) *B*	60 000	
Purchases (refreshments) *C*	25 000	
less Returns *D*	(5 000) deduct this from Purchases	
Total Stock available *E*	80 000	
less Closing Stock *F*	(40 000)	
Cost of Sales *G*	40 000	
Gross Profit *H*		160 000

Key to Picture House Ltd's trading account:

A **Sales revenue**: the total amount of money taken by the cinema over the year, from ticket sales, refreshments, etc. This is also called the **turnover**.

B **Opening stock**: the value of stock or goods left over from last year (the refreshments) that are available to sell at the beginning of the year.

C **Purchases**: the value of the new stock (new refreshments) bought during the year.

D **Returns**: the amount of money lost from damaged goods, such as crushed sweets or damaged cans, which could not be sold and had to be returned.

E **Total stock**: the total stock available is calculated from:

total stock =
    purchases – returns + opening stock

F **Closing stock**: the value of the stock (the refreshments) that have not been sold at the end of the year (31 December), when the trading account is worked out. This will then become the opening stock when the trading account is started for the next year. This is deducted from the total stock available.

G The **cost of sales** is calculated from:

cost of sales =
    total stock available – closing stock

H The **gross profit** is calculated by:

gross profit = sales revenue – cost of sales

(When calculated as a percentage of sales, this is called the **gross profit margin**.)

 TALK IT OVER

Using the figures below, together with the model shown for Picture House Ltd for 20X1, draw up the trading account to calculate the gross profit on refreshments for the company for 20X2.

Sales in 20X2   £240 000
Opening stock   £40 000
Purchases   £45 000
Returns   £5 000
Closing stock   £40 000

Calculate the gross profit for Picture House Ltd for 20X2.

What can you say about the performance of Picture House Ltd.

The **profit and loss account** shows how much net profit – or loss – the business has made over the previous financial year. The **net profit** is the actual profit the business has made, after all **overheads** – such as rent, rates, heating and lighting, and expenses such as office and vehicle expenses – have been paid. Net profit is calculated by deducting the overheads from the gross profit.

BUSINESS IN PRACTICE

Picture House Ltd made a gross profit of £160 000 in 20X1, but this was not the final profit, as all the overheads, such as the mortgage, rent, rates and wages, had not been taken into account. On the right is the trading and profit and loss account for Picture House Ltd.

Picture House Ltd
Trading and Profit and Loss Account year ending 31 December 20X1

	£	£	
Turnover (sales)		200 000	trading account
Cost of sales		40 000	
Gross profit		160 000	
Less overheads:			
Wages	60 000		profit & loss account
Rates/Insurance	10 000		
Heating and lighting	3 000		
Advertising	7 000		
Depreciation	7 000		
Administration	5 000		
Other expenses	8 000	100 000	
Net profit		60 000	

DEPRECIATION

Fixed assets fall in value over time, as they become worn out or obsolete. This drop in value is called **depreciation**, and is classified as an expense on the profit and loss account.

Depreciation can be calculated using the formula:

$$\text{annual depreciation} = \frac{\text{original value}[1] - \text{scrap value}[2]}{\text{life of asset (in yrs)}[3]}$$

For example, if Picture House Ltd bought projection equipment for £5000[1] and sold it for scrap 4 years[3] later at £1000[2], the annual depreciation would be:

$$\frac{£5000 - £1000}{4} = £1000$$

Fixed assets depreciate over time

PROFIT AND LOSS ACCOUNT FOR A PUBLIC LIMITED COMPANY

Profit and loss accounts for public limited companies include the details of at least the previous year, so that two years or more can be compared. There is less detailed information on costs, though this can vary from company to company.

The profit and loss account has three sections:

1 the **trading account** shows the gross profit
2 the **profit and loss account** is an extension of the trading account, and shows the net profit
3 the **appropriation account** shows how the profit has been used.

THE APPROPRIATION ACCOUNT

This section of the accounts shows how the net profit has been used by the company:

◆ **Tax on profits** – tax paid to the government.
◆ **Profit after tax** – profit left after paying taxes.
◆ **Dividends** – the amount that is paid to the shareholders, in dividends on their shares.
◆ **Retained profit** – money kept by the company to use for investment or expansion.

KEY POINTS

- **Profit and loss account** – a detailed account showing net profit or loss over a period of time.

- **Net profit** – profit after overheads and expenses have been deducted.

- A **profit and loss account** is divided into three sections:
  – trading account
  – profit and loss account
  – appropriation account.

- **Appropriation account** – an account that shows how the profit has been used by the company.

BUSINESS IN PRACTICE

A typical format for a profit and loss account is shown here. This account is for Wilton Sports plc, a public limited company.

TALK IT OVER

How does the profit and loss account for Wilton Sports plc differ from that for Picture House Ltd?

Wilton Sports plc
Profit and Loss Account
year ending 31 December 20X1

	20X1 £(1000)	20X0 £(1000)	
Turnover (sales)	1500	1400	trading account
Cost of sales	1000	100	
Gross profit	500	300	
Less expenses:			
Operating expenses	150	100	
Administration	40	20	profit & loss account
Distribution	25	10	
Depreciation	5	5	
Operating profit	280	165	
Interest receivable (payable)	(5)	(5)	
Net profit (Profit before taxation)	275	160	
Tax on profits	75	50	appropriation account
Profit after tax	200	110	
Dividends	100	60	
Retained profit	100	50	

TEST YOUR UNDERSTANDING ?

TOPICS 3–10

1 Why do businesses need finance?
2 Explain the difference between *internal* and *external* sources of finance.
3 What is an *overdraft*?
4 Give two examples of finance that could be used for *revenue expenditure*.
5 Give two examples of finance that could be used for *capital expenditure*.
6 Why do businesses keep accounts?
7 Explain in words how you would calculate: (a) cost of sales; (b) gross profit.
8 What is *closing stock*?
9 Why must depreciation be included in accounts as an expense?
10 What is the difference between *gross profit* and *net profit*?

CASE STUDY

Arsenal Football Club is a public limited company, and must publish its Annual Report and Accounts. Like many other business organisations, Arsenal makes its accounts available on the Internet. The Profit & Loss Account for the year ended 31 May 2000 is shown below.

PROFIT & LOSS ACCOUNT
for the year ended 31 May 2000

	2000 £(000)	1999 £(000)
Turnover	61,260	48,623
Costs and overheads less other income	(52,089)	(41,316)
Operating profit before player registation costs	9,171	7,307
Profit on sale of player registrations	22,216	2,061
Amortisation of player registrations	(10,172)	(7,300)
Profit on activities before taxation	21,215	2,068
Taxation	(7,105)	(760)
Profit after taxation retained for the financial year	14,110	1,308
Earnings per share	£251.96	£23.36

All trading resulted from continuing operations

1 Where would Arsenal's 'turnover' come from?
2 What costs and overheads might the club have?
3 Why are these figures in brackets?
4 In which year has Arsenal performed better?
5 What possible reasons could there be for Arsenal's success?

EXAM PRACTICE

Costa Ltd manufactures packaging products. The marketing director wants to make a wider range of packaging. A new machine costing £50 000 is needed to make this different packaging. The accountant estimates that the new £50 000 machine will be obsolete in five years and will then be worth only £5000.

1 Explain the difference between *assets* and *liabilities*. [2 marks]

2 Use examples to explain the difference between *fixed assets* and *current assets*. [4 marks]

3 Explain what is meant by *depreciation*. Use an example to illustrate your explanation. [3 marks]

4 Calculate the depreciation on the new machine. [3 marks]

5 Do you think Costa Ltd should buy the new machine? Give reasons for your answer. [4 marks]

6 The directors have decided to buy the new machine. How should Costa Ltd finance the purchase of the new machine? Give reasons for your answer. [4 marks]

Costa Ltd is a medium-sized manufacturer of packaging products. The business needs to buy an up-to-date computerised machine so that a wider range of packaging can be produced. Packaging machines are improving all the time, and the accountant estimates that the new £50 000 machine will be obsolete in five years and will then be worth only £5000.

1 'All assets are used up, wear out or become obsolete.' Explain carefully what this statement means. Use examples to illustrate your answer. [6 marks]

2 Considering the money that will be lost on the new machine, do you think that Costa Ltd would be right to buy it? Explain your answer. [4 marks]

3 The new machine can be funded by a share issue, by leasing, by hire purchase or by a bank loan. Discuss which source of finance would be the most appropriate. [10 marks]

The **balance sheet** gives details of the financial state of the business at a particular time. It shows what the business owns (**assets**) and what it owes (**liabilities**).

The balance sheet must **balance**, because the assets that the business buys must be paid for from the money it borrows, or from the business's own capital. The balance sheet can be used to calculate the business's **liquidity** – whether or not it can pay its debts.

The balance sheet and the profit and loss accounts can also be used together to see how **efficiently** the business is performing. For this a calculation is worked out on the **return on capital employed**. This shows how efficiently the business is using its capital to make profit.

INTERPRETING THE ACCOUNTS

The profit and loss account and the balance sheet must be included in the annual report and accounts of any business with private investors.

A balance sheet must balance

KEY POINTS

- **Balance sheet** – shows the financial state of the business as:
  - assets
  - liabilities
  - capital employed.

- **Net assets** must balance with capital employed.

- **Working capital** = current assets – current liabilities.

TALK IT OVER

On Picture House Ltd's balance sheet, net assets equal capital employed. Why must these figures balance?

BUSINESS IN PRACTICE

On the right is the balance sheet for Picture House Ltd.

THE BALANCE SHEET

A Fixed assets represents the value of all the assets that the business owns that are likely to stay within the business for one year or more (see Unit 5, Topic 3).

B Current assets represents the value of all the assets the business owns that are likely to last for *less* than one year.

C Creditors represents a **current liability**. In this case it is a sum that the business owes and must repay within one year. Examples are an **overdraft** or **trade credit** (see Unit 5, Topic 2). The figure is in brackets because it must be *taken away*, not added.

D Net current assets =
    current assets – current liabilities

This represents the finance available for the day-to-day running of the business. It is also called **working capital**.

E Creditors represents a long-term liability. In this case it is a sum that the business owes and must repay after one year. Examples are a **mortgage** or a **debenture** (see Unit 5, Topic 6).

F Net assets = fixed assets + net current assets – long-term liabilities

or

Net assets = fixed assets + current assets – current liabilities – long-term liabilities

CAPITAL AND RESERVES

G Called-up share capital represents the value of the shares sold by the business when it started.

H Share premium account represents the value of the shares issued later on, at a

Picture House Ltd
Balance Sheet as at 31 December 20X2

	£(000)	
Fixed assets		
Tangible assets	500	
Investments	20	
	520	A
Current assets		
Stocks	60	
Debtors	20	
Cash	100	
	180	B
Current liabilities		
Creditors: amounts falling due within one year	(100)	C
Net current assets (Current assets – current liabilities)	80	D
Total assets less current liabilities	600	
Long-term liabilities		
Creditors: amounts falling due after one year	(150)	E
Net assets	450	F
Capital and reserves		
Called-up share capital	300	G
Share premium account	30	H
Other reserves	20	I
Profit and loss account	100	J
Capital employed	450	K

higher value, perhaps to finance new technology or expansion.

I Other reserves represents other money in the business – it may be that the business owns the property, and the value of this property has increased over the years.

J Profit and loss account represents the total amount of profit that has been kept by the business over the years, instead of paying it in dividends to the shareholders. This amount is 'transferred' from the profit and loss account.

K The final line of the balance sheet shows the **capital employed** by the business: this must balance with the **net assets**.

The profit and loss account and the balance sheet are used to calculate the business's **liquidity** (its ability to pay its debts), its **profitability** (how much profit is made from sales), and how **efficiently** it is using its capital. Below are some of the formulae used in these calculations.

CURRENT RATIO

The current ratio shows anyone who is interested in the business's accounts how easily it is able to pay its current liabilities out of its current assets – in other words, how easily it can pay its short-term debts:

$$\text{current ratio} = \frac{\text{current assets}}{\text{current}}$$

For a healthy business, current ratios should be between 1.5 and 2.0. For example, the current ratio for Picture House Ltd is:

$$\frac{\text{current assets}}{\text{current}} = \frac{180}{100} = 1.8$$

This means that Picture House Ltd, should it need to pay off the liabilities, has 1.8 times the amount of current assets to current liabilities. This tells someone looking at the balance sheet that the business is in a healthy position. In fact, it could reduce its current assets or increase its current liabilities and still remain in a healthy position.

ACID-TEST RATIO

The acid-test ratio is another test of the business's ability to pay off its current liabilities. With acid tests, stocks are not included in the calculation, as these may not always be sold within the current year – they are not as liquid as other current assets.

$$\text{acid-test ratio} = \frac{\text{current assets} - \text{stock}}{\text{current liabilities}}$$

Picture House Ltd's acid-test ratio is:

$$\frac{\text{current assets} - \text{stock}}{\text{current liabilities}} = \frac{180 - 60}{100} = \frac{120}{100} = 1.2$$

Acid-test ratios should be between 0.8 and 1.0. This

 TALK IT OVER

Which aspect of a business do you think is the most important – its profitability or its liquidity?

To find the figures for current assets, liabilities, stocks and capital employed, a business needs to look back at its balance sheet.

ratio shows that Picture House Ltd is able to pay its current liabilities, straight away, from its current assets. Again the figure is a little higher than it need be: the business could afford to reduce current assets or increase current liabilities, and would still remain healthy.

PROFITABILITY RATIOS

Two ratios can be used to see how well the business is turning sales revenue into profit. They are **gross profit margin** and **net profit margin**:

$$\text{gross profit margin} = \frac{\text{gross profit}}{\text{sales}} \times 100\%$$

$$\text{net profit margin} = \frac{\text{net profit}}{\text{sales}} \times 100\%$$

For Picture House Ltd:

$$\text{gross profit margin} = \frac{160}{200} \times 100\% = 80\%$$

$$\text{net profit margin} = \frac{60}{200} \times 100\% = 30\%$$

These figures mean that for every £1 Picture House Ltd receives in sales revenue, 80p becomes gross profit, and 30p then becomes net profit.

Businesses try to achieve the highest percentage possible for both gross profit margin and net profit margin. A large difference between the two ratios means that the business is spending a lot of its revenue on overheads or expenses.

RETURN ON CAPITAL EMPLOYED

The **return on capital employed** (**ROCE**) formula shows how efficiently the business is using its capital to make a profit. This uses data from the profit and loss account and the balance sheet.

$$\text{return on capital employed} = \frac{\text{operating profit}}{\text{capital}}$$

Picture House Ltd's return on capital employed is:

$$\frac{\text{operating profit}}{\text{capital}} = \frac{100}{450} \times 100\% = 22.2\%$$

In simple terms, this means that for every £1 invested in the company, 22.2p profit is generated. The higher this figure, the better the capital in the business is doing its work.

TALK IT OVER

To be able to comment on the performance of Picture House Ltd, what other information would you need?

Ratios alone may not provide enough information to judge how well a business is performing. A number of other ways of measuring a business's success may also be considered.

SIZE

If a business is **growing**, this means that the business has been successful in achieving **expansion**. Size can be measured in the following ways.

Sales revenue

The **sales revenue** (**turnover**) will increase if the business gains more customers. More customers indicate that the business is coping well with the competition.

Profit

Profits depend on sales, so increasing sales will usually lead to increased profits. Bigger profits make more funds available for further expansion.

Number of employees

As sales increase, more **employees** are needed to meet the greater demand.

Assets

As the business grows, more assets are needed – for example, more buildings or more machinery. These additional assets give the business a greater capacity to grow further still.

Calculation of the year-on-year percentage change gives a **rate of growth**

MARKET SHARE

Market share is the business's percentage of the total market. For example, if a business had a 75% market share of the UK hamburger market, this would mean that that business sold 75% of *all* hamburgers sold in the UK:

$$\text{market share} = \frac{\text{business's sales}}{\text{total market}} \times 100\% = \frac{75}{100} = 75\%$$

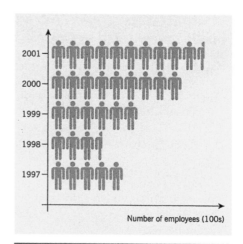

Number of employees (100s)

More employees are needed as sales increase

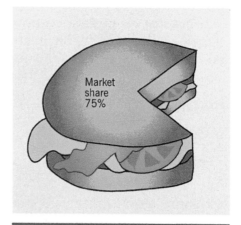

Market share 75%

Market share is the business's percentage of the total market

Surveys can be used to gauge customer satisfaction

KEY POINTS

■ Businesses can measure performance by size, by market share, and by customer feedback.

■ Growth can be measured by changes in sales revenue, profit, number of employees, and assets.

CUSTOMER FEEDBACK

The final test of a business's performance is whether the customer is happy. Businesses such as Asda carry out customer satisfaction surveys; others monitor the number of customer complaints. Depending on the feedback, the business can take action to improve its product or service.

BUSINESS IN PRACTICE

Originally Alton Towers was a stately home, but it was converted to a theme park in the 1980s. Its original big thrill ride was 'The Corkscrew'. At the time, 'The Corkscrew' was as famous as 'Oblivion' is today.

Since the launch of 'The Corkscrew', Alton Towers has seen more than 40 million visitors. It is now Britain's number-one theme park, with more visitors than any other park in Britain (more than 2.5 million visitors every year).

In one recent year, Alton Towers had 1800 seasonal staff and 300 full-time staff, who were employed in roles such as ride operators, security officers and events organisers.

The theme park is situated in 500 acres of land, and every year millions of pounds are spent developing a new ride or improving some aspect of the park.

 TALK IT OVER

In what ways could you say that Alton Towers was a successful business? What additional information would help you to decide exactly *how* successful the theme park is?

TEST YOUR UNDERSTANDING

TOPICS 11–13

1 Why is it important to measure the performance of a business?
2 How would you calculate the current ratio for a business?
3 A business has an acid-test ratio of 0.3. Comment on this figure.
4 What can the ROCE ratio tell us about a business?
5 Why do businesses compare ratios from different years?
6 What is working capital?
7 How would you calculate working capital?
8 Explain the difference between *fixed assets* and *current assets*.
9 Explain the difference between an *asset* and a *liability*.
10 Which two figures on a balance sheet must balance?

CASE STUDY

Arsenal Football Club plc publishes its Annual Report and Accounts on the Internet. Its balance sheet on 31 May 2000 is shown opposite.

1 Which two figures balance?
2 What fixed assets might the club own?
3 Which two items also appear on the trading and profit and loss account?
4 Calculate liquidity ratios (current ratio and acid-test ratio) for 1999 and 2000. In which year was the club in a healthier state?
5 Calculate ROCE for 1999 and 2000. In which year is the figure better?

ARSENAL FOOTBALL CLUB PLC
Annual Report and Accounts, 1999-2000

BALANCE SHEET

31 May 2000

	2000			1999
	£(000)	£(000)	£(000)	£(000)
Fixed assets				
Tangible assets		36,491		33,378
Intangible assets		38,832		27,469
		75,323		60,847
Current assets				
Stocks	582		383	
Debtors	9,586		1,633	
Debtors: amounts recoverable in more than one year	12,000		–	
Cash at bank and in hand	7,261		13,464	
	29,429		15,480	
Creditors: amounts falling due within one year	(33,995)		(27,491)	
Net current liabilities		4,566		12,011
Total assets less current (liabilities)		70,757		48,836
Creditors: amounts falling due after more than one year		(25,749)		(18,038)
Provisional for liabilities & charges		(3,930)		(3,830)
Net assets		41,078		26,968
Equity capital and reserves				
Called-up equity share capital		56		56
Share premium account		237		237
Profit and loss account		40,785		26,675
Equity shareholders' funds		41,078		26,968

Business plans

Having reached the end of the book, it will be helpful to consider why all of the topics that have been discussed are important to businesses.

Whenever a business is started, it is important to prepare a **business plan**. A common saying emphasises the importance of such plans: 'A business that is not successful has not planned to fail, but has failed to plan.'

THE PURPOSE OF THE BUSINESS PLAN

When a business starts up, or is going to expand, the business plan will show how the business's objectives are to be achieved. The business plan is needed in raising finance, as it can be used to explain to potential lenders how the business will be run. A business plan increases the chance of survival, because if the plan has not been thoroughly thought out, problems in it may be identified and resolved at this stage.

When the business is up and running, the business plan will provide a framework, enabling managers to monitor the business and take action if something does not go as planned.

THE CONTENT OF THE BUSINESS PLAN

The style and structure of business plans will differ between organisations, but all business plans have the same kind of content. A suggested plan might include the following:

Details of the business

Information about the business such as:

◆ business name, address, etc.
◆ the type of ownership
◆ the size of the business
◆ any special features, such as key customers or suppliers
◆ possible problems and how they will be solved, such as getting planning permission, or operating with a single currency.

Objectives of the business

All the goals of the business.

Personnel

An organisation chart could be provided, with additional information about the employees, such as their qualifications, ages, experience, and lengths of service. The entrepreneur might also include information about incentives and payment systems.

Business activity

Descriptions of what the business produces, and of how the product or service differs from those of similar businesses.

Production

Details such as:

- production methods to be used
- availability of raw materials
- possible suppliers
- quality assurance
- location issues.

Marketing

Details such as:

- potential customers – and the market research evidence that they will exist
- the price of the product or service, and the basis for this decision
- promotion – how the customers will be persuaded to buy
- distribution
- customer service and after-sales service.

Finance

A new business will include forecast financial information, whereas an existing business can also include past information. This will be in the form of:

- a profit and loss account
- a cash-flow forecast
- a balance sheet
- a break-even chart
- a statement of the finance needed and how it will be used.

KEY POINTS

- A business plan is used:
  - to convince lenders that it is safe to provide finance for the business
  - to test the entrepreneur's business idea
  - to monitor the progress of the business.

- A business plan covers the whole of the GCSE Business Studies course!

The future

The business plan will also include the ambitions of the business, for example an idea of how it intends to grow.

BUSINESS IN PRACTICE

Business plans are so important that Microsoft includes a 'wizard' in its PowerPoint program, to help entrepreneurs prepare and present their business plans.

ACTIVITY

If you have access to PowerPoint, you could try to produce your own business plan, using the AutoContentsWizard.

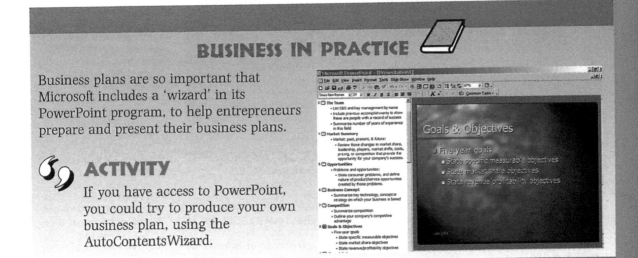

Index